Advance praise for *Second Quarter*

"Wow! What a valuable and important book David Cottrell has penned. I read it in two sittings and now have a marked-up, underlined copy. You'll feel the same way. It's that good."

Pat Williams
Co-founder and senior vice president of the NBA's Orlando Magic,
Author of *21 GREAT LEADERS*

"During our second quarter, we begin to understand that life is not all about us. And, our influence is incredibly powerful whether we recognize it or not. This book will take you through the steps that will allow you to live life to the fullest. Read it, and then give it to a friend."

Reagan Lambert
Director, Fellowship of Christian Athletes

"David Cottrell tackles the tough obstacles typical of the second quarter of life with an ease of language and depth of insight we've come to expect from him. David's wisdom and personal experience are great resources for those who hope to do more than simply survive until halftime. This book will help you thrive."

Denny Rydberg
President, Young Life

"David Cottrell's words are an eternal gift to me and you. *Second Quarter* is a survival kit for everyone who dreams big and hopes fully. It will inspire you to not only hold on, but prosper through the challenges of the game of life."

David L. Cook
Author/Executive Producer of *Seven Days in Utopia*

Second Quarter

Get the *most*
out of life's
toughest times

David Cottrell

CornerStone
Leadership Institute

Second Quarter

Get the Most out of Life's Toughest Times

Printed in the United States of America.

ISBN: 978-0-9961469-0-6

Published by: CornerStone Leadership Institute
P.O. Box 76408
Dallas, TX 75376
972.298.8377

Credits
Copy Editor — Jami Wilmarth, Amarillo, TX

Design, Art Direction, and Production — Melissa Cabana, Back Porch Creative, Frisco, TX
melissa@backporchcreative.com

Table of Contents

Introduction

It's game day

The autumn afternoon is cool and crisp — a perfect day for football. Outside the stadium, pop-up tents and lawn chairs pepper the campus landscape. Friends catch up on the latest news in each other's lives. Kids throw footballs and Frisbees, and pitch beanbags. The aroma of grilling hamburgers, ribs and chicken fills the air. Our fight song blares through speakers from every direction. Glancing across the way, a sea of red proudly waves as our fans wear school colors. Emotions run high. Electricity is in the air.

Today our team plays the No. 1 team in the country. We are ready. Our fans eagerly anticipate an unforgettable game. The coaches have prepared tirelessly. Optimism and confidence abound. Today is our day.

The stadium fills to capacity. We enthusiastically yell at the top of our voices and fanatically wave our red and white shakers as our team runs onto the field. We hardly can hear ourselves think through the noise. The opponent's small groups of fans yell encouragement to their team, but the noise of our fans drowns out their cheers. We have a definite home-field advantage, and we are convinced that all the pieces will fall right into place for a big win.

Game time

The first quarter begins, and we dominate the best team in the country. Our noisy, passionate fans' enthusiasm has carried onto the field. Our team is playing its best — just like we planned and hoped.

Early in the game, we connect on a couple of big plays and capture the momentum. Maybe this game might not be as difficult as everyone thought. Our team's exhaustive preparation is paying off. We have the lead! The scoreboard shines 7-0 with the good guys ahead at the end of the first quarter. All indications are that today is, indeed, our day.

The second quarter begins. Suddenly, the visitors drive 80 yards to tie the score. Seemingly out of nowhere things began to feel different. Reality begins to set in: The No. 1 team is bigger, faster and stronger than it appeared in the first quarter. All of the preparation for the game did not reveal how incredibly athletic the opponent's team really is. The crowd is shocked into silence as the visitors dominate the second quarter. Panic sets in. We have got to get to halftime so we can make adjustments to get us back in the game. Hang on team! We can adjust! Hang on!

The halftime score is 7-28.

During halftime, our coaches make adjustments. The teams play evenly the rest of the game, but the second quarter proved too much for our team to overcome. At the end of the game, few fans remain in the stands. The pregame excitement turned into postgame questions, disappointment and frustration. If only we had gotten to halftime before the score got out of hand! What if the adjustments that worked so well in the third and fourth quarters had been made during the second quarter?

What if … what if …

Getting to Halftime

Several years ago, I read a book titled, "Halftime," by Bob Buford. The book had a profound impact on me at "halftime" in my life. Buford wrote about living a life of excellence during the second half of life. He challenged readers to move from *success to significance*. The book provided me with direction and encouragement as I approached *my* second half.

Since then, I have worked with and mentored many people living in the second quarter of their lives. Regardless of age, they struggle to hang on until halftime. They believe that if they can just make it to halftime …

Using the football game analogy, in the pregame of your life, you prepare to attack the real world. You study, observe, take tests and evaluate your progress. You learn how to get along with people from different backgrounds. You probably discover that special person with whom you want to spend the rest of your life. You date. You have fun together. You can't wait until you exchange vows to love each other "for better or for worse" forever.

The wedding day arrives. You and your true love are about to enter your first quarter together. Excitement fills the air. Your friends and family gather to celebrate, encourage and throw rice at you as you begin your blissful life together. You are in the game. You are in the first quarter together. Nothing can stop you. Your enthusiasm for each other and for life will overcome anything life throws your way. Bring it on!

The second quarter *does* bring it on.

During the second quarter, your honeymoon becomes a distant memory. Suddenly, you face the unexpected realities of life. You might hear words you never thought would apply to you:

- ✦ "Your mortgage payment is past due."
- ✦ "We are cutting back, and your job is no longer required."

You could experience things you never imagined would apply to you:

- ✦ You say your final goodbye to a loved one.
- ✦ You receive a devastating diagnosis from a doctor.
- ✦ Your children make decisions that disappoint you.
- ✦ You burn out.

Many times, the second quarter ends tragically — even for wonderful, God-loving people. Marriages die. People commit suicide. Jobs become stale and unfulfilling. Pornography is attractive and addictive. Families feud and take sides over issues that destroy relationships of lifelong friends. Alcohol becomes a new best friend. Depression feels normal. You may be filled with guilt or loneliness.

You never intended to be where you are, but somehow, life's pressures blitzed you. Halftime seems forever away.

How do you get to halftime? What adjustments can you make right now — before things get worse? Can you hang on? Is it already too late?

No. It is not too late. It is never too late.

Second quarter struggles are not unique to you; we all experience them. Solomon wrote several thousands of years ago: "*What has been will be again, what has been done will be done again; there is nothing new under the sun. Is there anything of which one can say, Look! This is something new? It was here already, long ago; it was here before our time.*"[1]

Regardless of the second quarter challenge consuming your time and energy, it is not new and you are not alone.

The apostle Paul provided us a second quarter warning followed by second-quarter encouragement: *"No temptation has seized you except what is common to man. And God is faithful; he will not let you be tempted beyond what you can bear. But when you are tempted, he will also provide a way out so that you can stand up under it."*[2]

No matter what struggle you face, God is faithful. He will provide a way out. No matter where you are or how you got there, you can make adjustments to prevent the second quarter from destroying your dreams.

You might ask how long your second quarter will last. I don't know. But, I *do* know you can survive your second quarter and live the rest of your life fully with faith, hope and love — regardless of what the second quarter has brought on.

You can hang on!

Spiritual game planning

Many people spend more time planning a weeklong vacation than planning their eternal future. The purpose of this book is to help you create a spiritual life plan to get the most out of your second quarter and beyond. It is written about people who discovered that hope and help were available to them.

It is to you, as well.

Jesus said, "*You will know the truth, and the truth will set you free!*"[3] Freedom comes from understanding God's word and living your life based on biblical truth. "*Everything that was written in the past was written to teach us, so that through endurance and encouragement of the scriptures we might have hope.*"[4] Your freedom and your hope come from understanding what the scriptures say about how to prepare yourself, prosper during, and help others through their second quarter.

While it's okay to read this book alone, remember you are *not* alone in the second quarter. Look around you. Every person within your sight will be, has been or is in his or her second quarter. Every person.

Life's challenges, opportunities and victories are best shared with others. I suggest you find a few people to read this book with you. Invite people who are willing to devote their time with you so you can improve your lives together. Making changes is easier when you support one another along the way.

Discussion questions are provided at the end of each chapter to facilitate your conversation. More important, you will be investing in each other. Your inspiration and encouragement will fill each other with renewed courage, spirit and hope as you work through the second quarter together.

"When you pass through the waters,
I will be with you;
and when you pass through the rivers,
they will not sweep over you.
When you walk through the fire,
you will not be burned,
the flames will not set you ablaze."
– Isaiah 43:2

PART ONE

Preparing for Your Second Quarter

"As for everyone who comes to me and hears my words
and puts them into practice, I will show you what they are like.
They are like a man building a house,
who dug down deep and laid the foundation on rock.
When a flood came, the torrent struck that house
but could not shake it, because it was well built."
– Luke 6:47

chapter 1

Dig Your Faith Well Deep

"And without faith it is impossible to please God, because anyone who comes to him must believe that he exists and that he rewards those who earnestly seek him."

– HEBREWS 11:6

Your second quarter can produce some of the greatest moments of your life. Wonderful events probably will happen: The birth of your children, the beginning of your career, promotions, new neighborhoods, new friends and new adventures.

Along with those great, exciting moments will come some challenges. Guaranteed. That is why you need to dig your faith well deep while in the first quarter — before your second-quarter tests unexpectedly show up.

The Bible says that faith is, "*confidence in what we hope for and assurance about what we do not see.*"[1] Your human nature is to want to know the unknown and see the unseen. If you could do that, you would not need faith. Faith is the ability to make the not yet as real as the already.

Active faith is not up for negotiation: "*Without faith it is impossible to please God because anyone who comes to him must believe that he exists and that he rewards those who earnestly seek him.*"[2] There is no wiggle room: Without faith, you cannot please God. Your personal vision should be as Paul's: "*I have fought the good fight, I have finished the race, **I have kept the faith.***"[3] Regardless of what happens or why it happens, your mission is to keep your faith.

A well too shallow

A good friend of mine grew up with his family on a relatively small ranch in Texas. The homestead was the site of a lifetime of great childhood memories for him and his siblings. A well on their property provided the ranch's water that filled the family's buckets and supplied its home with water. Even during the worst Texas droughts, the well never ran dry.

In the flash of a moment, though, things changed. Early one summer evening, a fire broke out in the attic. The family ran to its water supply, moved the hose into the attic and began fighting the fire. The fire gained momentum in the dry, dusty attic. Thirty minutes into the fire, just before quenching the flames, the well lost water pressure. Never before had the water supply run out, but on this night, the well ran dry.

The family's well simply was not deep enough to handle the unexpected emergency. Their home was destroyed.

The first question before drilling any well is, "how deep do we drill?" The depth of the well requires a detailed, long-range plan before digging. Water tables fluctuate up and down, so the driller must drill deeper than the lowest-expected water level. In addition, unexpected water consumption may occur; family needs may change, or you may need the water to irrigate your land.

Of course, a deeper well takes more time and costs more to drill than a shallow well. However, not drilling deep enough in the beginning can result in problems later that will be much more expensive to fix.

The worst thing that could happen is what happened to my friend: The well went dry when needed the most.

Dig deep

During life's journey, you will find it necessary to dig deep into your faith well. The thought may not be pleasant, but life will test your faith. If your faith reservoir is full, you probably will be able draw from that well and prevent a catastrophe in your life.

When things are going well, having faith is easy; your well overflows. You handle situations pretty easily because great times do not test your faith. Everything is good! It is easy to "*live by faith, not by sight*"[4] when your faith is not tested.

However, when a faith test comes along, everybody struggles. Even the disciples — who saw Jesus perform miracles firsthand — struggled with their faith. They witnessed miracle after miracle and even preached to others about Jesus' miracles. Yet, when personally faced with danger, fear, unknown circumstances and unexpected trials, their faith waivered. Think of some of the astonishing events they witnessed:

- Five thousand people fed with five loaves and two fish[5]
- Jesus calmed the winds and sea[6]
- Demons jumped from a man into pigs[7]
- The sick healed[8]
- The paralyzed walked[9]
- Lepers healed[10]
- Jesus walked on water[11]
- Blind men saw[12]

- ✦ Mute men spoke[13]
- ✦ Dead men lived[14]
- ✦ Water turned to wine[15]
- ✦ A man's ear restored[16]
- ✦ A lame man healed[17]

After the disciples saw Jesus perform those miracles, you would think their faith never would waiver. However, the 12 men closest to Jesus still struggled with their faith.

Jesus questioned them, "*Why are you still afraid? Do you still have no faith?*"[18] Even after all they had witnessed, fear trumped their faith. No wonder you have to work so hard at growing in faith.

To grow in faith, you must consistently dig your well before a crisis occurs. Because,"*without faith it is impossible to please God,*"[19] your top priority should be to become more faithful. The Bible directs you to "*consider it pure joy my brothers when you face trials of many kinds, because you know the testing of our faith develops perseverance.*"[20]

Are you kidding? Joy when facing trials? Did anyone ask for more perseverance?

Why do you struggle to live the abundant life that God has provided for you? You may be in the same boat as Paul when he admitted: "*I do not understand what I do. For what I want to do, I do not do, but what I hate I do.*"[21] I certainly face that struggle. Sometimes my faith well dries up, and I have to bring in reinforcements to help me dig deeper.

You may be at a great place in your life. I hope so. That is the time to dig your faith well deeper. I hope you never have to draw from the depths of the well, but start digging just in case.

Or, you currently might be in a faith drought. If so, it is not too late to begin digging. The water is there if you seek it and dig deep enough.

Dig your well by taking a look inside

How deep is your faith well right now? Is it deep enough to draw from, if needed? Is developing your faith a priority in your life? Do you have trusted spiritual advisors to help you make tough decisions? Do you have a plan to follow when your faith test appears?

God allows you to choose: Do you trust Him, or not? Are you bold enough to serve Him, or not? Are you humble enough to submit to His will and timing, or not?

You must answer these questions before your faith test unexpectedly appears. If you have a solid plan, trust Him, serve Him already, and are humble to His will, you will be better equipped to face any test that comes along.

You will share the same feelings as Paul expressed: "*We are pressed on every side by troubles, but we are not crushed. We are perplexed, but not driven to despair. We are hunted down, but never abandoned by God. We get knocked down, but we are not destroyed.*"[22]

Life may knock you down, but God will never abandon you. No matter what faith test you experience, it has value. Faith tests are a necessary part of your life as you become complete.

Take a look inside. Is your faith well deep enough to draw from when your faith test suddenly appears?

Full accounting

The Bible is clear about being accountable to God: "*Nothing in all creation is hidden from God's sight. Everything is uncovered and laid bare before the eyes of him to whom we must give account.*"[23] Ultimately, you will have to give account for every area of your life.

Jesus taught accountability in a parable about talents.[24] As the story goes, the master divided talents among his servants according to their abilities. Of the three men given talents, the man receiving the most talents put the talents to work and gained more. Another man was given fewer talents and put his talents to work to gain more. The third man dug a hole in the ground, hid his talent and chose not to put the talent to work. The two who accepted their responsibility were described as *good and faithful*. The one who did not was described as *wicked and lazy*; he lost the talent he had been given.

Good and faithful, or wicked and lazy. These are your choices; they depend on what you do with what you have been given. The question is not *how much* you have, but *what you do* with what you have.

When you become fully accountable to God, you may have to make changes. You lose the right to blame others for your spiritual condition. Regardless of the past, it is not your parents, friends, priest or pastor who can improve your situation now or in the future.

Being fully accountable also means you lose the right to be negative or cynical about God's gift of life. And, being fully accountable means you become fully committed to doing God's work.

In a nutshell, you are accountable for everything you control — and you control whether you live a life of active faith. The more energy you exert digging your faith well deep, the more you will be able to positively influence those around you.

Dig your well by reflecting Christ

Regardless of the circumstance — whether your well is overflowing or bone dry — you are responsible for others seeing Jesus in you. This holds true during good times or bad.

My late wife, Karen, dug her faith well deep. She believed — without a shadow of doubt — that, "*all things work together for the good for those who love Him and have been called according to His purpose.*"[25]

For 12 years, she battled a rare and aggressive cancer. Given her circumstances, most would have been bitter and angry with God.

Karen believed in God's plan for her life and learned to live an abundant life with cancer, instead of to die a bitter life from cancer. Throughout her illness, she leaned on one of her favorite verses from the Bible: "*For I know the plans I have for you, declares the Lord, plans to prosper you and not to harm you, plans to give you hope and a future.*"[26] She did not live in fear of dying. She lived in hope and faith of living eternally.

She believed that when God called her home, it would be His timing, fulfilling His plan. Cancer could not take a day from her life. *God* had the timing in control. She knew God would not be surprised when she showed up. He knew it was her time, and He welcomed her home with open arms.

People often asked her how she could live joyfully while battling a horrible disease. She always was quick to share her faith. On several occasions, people told her they saw Jesus through her strong, confident faith.

Ironically, she frequently talked about seeing Jesus in others. Karen loved angels — small willow tree angels decorated our home. More importantly, she saw Jesus through the many angels on earth. She saw Jesus in our neighbors and friends who brought food. She saw Jesus in the people who sat with her during chemo treatments. She saw Jesus when a friend knelt to visit and pray with her. She saw Jesus when her friends traveled long distances to spend a few minutes with her in her last days. She saw Jesus when the church choir came to our home to sing for her. She saw Jesus when a nurse comforted her. She saw Jesus when people prayed for her. She even said she could hear prayers for her and could repeat many of the prayers that were said.

She saw Jesus in people like you — God's chosen angels in her life.

I believe she saw Jesus in those around her because, like looking in a mirror, those around her saw Jesus' reflection in her. Karen glorified God in everything she did. For years, she encouraged others. In her time of need, she continued to encourage others by allowing them to care for her. She reflected Jesus equally during her time of suffering as during her time of good health.

During her last days on earth, Karen drifted toward God's arms, not with fear and bitterness, but with peace and hope. She taught all those around her not how to *die*, but how to *live*.

She dug her faith well deep by honoring God with her reflection.

Dig your well by encouraging others

You can dig your faith well deep by encouraging others. No matter how successful, positive, secure or mature a person might seem, genuine encouragement never fails to help. In fact, all people need encouragement. As a side benefit, the more you encourage others, the more you are encouraged yourself.

The Bible says, "*Let us hold fast the confession of our hope without wavering, for He who promised is faithful, and let us consider how to stimulate one another to love and good deeds, not forsaking our own assembling together, as is the habit of some but encouraging one another...*"[27]

One of the greatest ways of encouraging others is to lift them up in prayer and help them. It is easy — and maybe natural — to become discouraged along life's journey. The world is full of discouragers. However, we have a duty to encourage one another, and we all can do it.

I can hear you saying, "But the people I am around are not encouraging. In fact, they are discouraging, so how can I be a positive encourager?" Good question. I know exactly what you mean. Sometimes it is frustrating, but search for ways to encourage them, and maybe the situation will change. Here is how:

"*Therefore* ***encourage*** *one another and* ***build each other up****, just as in fact you are doing. Now we ask you, brothers, to* ***respect*** *those who work hard among you, who are over you in the Lord and who admonish you. Hold them in the highest regard in love because of their work.* ***Live in peace*** *with each other. And we urge you, brothers,* ***warn those who are idle, encourage the timid, help the weak, be patient with everyone****. Make sure that nobody pays back wrong for wrong, but always try to* ***be kind to each other*** *and to everyone else.* ***Be joyful always; pray continually; give thanks in all circumstances****, for this is God's will for you in Christ Jesus. Do not put out the Spirit's fire; do not treat prophecies with contempt. Test everything.* ***Hold on to the good. Avoid every kind of evil.*** *May God himself, the God of peace, sanctify you through and through.*"[28]

That is quite a comprehensive list of ways to encourage those around you. Pick two or three from the list, and try them. You might be surprised who becomes more encouraged.

Summary

Your faith is not up for negotiation: "*Without faith it is impossible to please God.*"[29]

The Bible tells us that even many of the most faithful people were not able to see the result of their faith firsthand. "*All these people were still living by faith when they died. They did not receive the things promised; they only saw them and welcomed them from a distance.*"[30]

Even if you have to welcome your faith from a distance, it is up to you to follow God's plan. That plan requires you to dig your well deep by living your faith actively, taking a close look inside yourself, reflecting Jesus to those around you, and encouraging others.

Dig your faith well deep right now, even if you are not thirsty. That is the best time to dig.

Questions for Discussion

- ✦ How do you know when you are in your second quarter? What happens during that time? What are the potential outcomes of the second quarter?
- ✦ In what areas of your life is your faith being tested right now? How are you responding?
- ✦ What is the lesson you can apply from the parable of the talents?
- ✦ Do you see Christ reflected in people around you? What does that reflection look like?
- ✦ Are others seeing Christ reflected in you? What does your reflection look like?
- ✦ Reflecting on the passage about encouraging, can you think of some specific ways for you to encourage others around you today?

chapter 2

Guard Your Integrity

"My lips shall not speak wickedness,
nor my tongue utter deceit."
– Job 27:4

Many times, especially during the second quarter, you will face an integrity test. It may involve your career, your family or a personal decision ... but temptation to sacrifice your integrity will come. It will probably appear like a pop quiz, when you least expect it.

Facing an integrity test is never pleasant, even when you think you are prepared. Establishing and protecting a foundation of integrity is essential for living a Godly life. If you sacrifice your integrity, you risk losing everything before you get to halftime. Living with integrity is a better way.

Most people recognize integrity when they see it, but it can be tough to describe. Typically, people use the words integrity and honesty interchangeably. However, integrity is a much broader term that comes from the word *integral*, which means whole or undivided. If you have integrity, you are a *complete* person; your character is undivided. Without integrity, you are an incomplete person; your actions are inconsistent.

Integrity is the master switch that controls every part of your life. It doesn't matter what you say to people if they don't trust you. It doesn't matter how committed, optimistic, skilled or courageous you are if people do not believe you.

Without integrity, you eventually will be alone; everyone will flee from you.

How important is integrity?

When you install a new software program on your computer, it automatically runs an "integrity check" — a series of tests to determine whether any part of the program has been lost or damaged. If any piece of the code in that program doesn't have complete integrity, the program as a whole can't be trusted. At best, the program will not function properly. At worst, using a program lacking integrity could cause valuable data loss or even computer damage; the integrity check is absolutely necessary.

Your integrity check — constantly asking yourself, "Am I consistent in my words and action?" — is required for long-term success in all areas of your life. When people know what to expect from you, they can trust you.

Trust is a byproduct of integrity. If you are trustworthy and hold true to your word and convictions, people will want to be with you. Everyone wants to be with those whose audio (words) syncs with their video (actions), and who have proven themselves honest and trustworthy. People yearn for consistency in which values do not change based on recent circumstances.

If you sacrifice your integrity, you risk losing everything. Take a look:

Integrity breach — everyone is vulnerable

General David Petraeus was brilliant. After graduating in the top five percent of his class in the United States Military Academy at West Point, his career skyrocketed. He spent 37 years in the Army and was promoted to a Four Star General. He is credited for drafting the plan for the "surge," which stabilized post-Saddam Iraq and, at one time, seemed a model for future warfare.

In 2011, shortly after the successful surge, General Petraeus became director of the CIA, confirmed with a Senate vote of 94 to 0. He was one of the most admired people in America. He was even considered as a potential presidential candidate.

On Nov. 9, 2012, everything changed. He wrote the following letter to his subordinates:[1]

> "Yesterday afternoon, I went to the White House and asked the President to be allowed, for personal reasons, to resign from my position as D/CIA. After being married for over 37 years, I showed extremely poor judgment by engaging in an extramarital affair. Such behavior is unacceptable, both as a husband and as the leader of an organization such as ours. This afternoon, the President graciously accepted my resignation.
>
> "As I depart Langley, I want you to know that it has been the greatest of privileges to have served with you, the officers of our Nation's Silent Service, a work force that is truly exceptional in every regard. Indeed, you did extraordinary work on a host of critical missions during my time as director, and I am deeply grateful to you for that.
>
> "Teddy Roosevelt once observed that life's greatest gift is the opportunity to work hard at work worth doing. I will always treasure my opportunity to have done that with you and I will

always regret the circumstances that brought that work with you to an end."

A stellar career ended that day. One of our country's greatest leaders — in his own words — "showed extremely poor judgment," exhibited "unacceptable behavior," and "will always regret" his integrity breach.

Brilliant was not the adjective used to describe David Petraeus after Nov. 9, 2012.

How could that happen? How could a great strategist, brilliant mind and powerful leader lose control of his personal life? How could he sacrifice his career and family?

If you are not careful, the same could happen to you. No one is immune to an integrity breach.

Integrity out of the news

Integrity is a hot news item. Check any news source, and you will find more than ample evidence that serious problems exist with integrity. Unfortunately, lack of integrity has become so prevalent that many have become calloused to it. Are you surprised anymore to discover a politician lacks integrity? Truth be known, you actually may expect it. Every day you see, hear and read of integrity breaches.

We easily can criticize obvious, news-making breaches in integrity, such as with General Petraeus. However, we may want to check ourselves before we jump on the criticism bandwagon and begin casting out stones. Most integrity mistakes never make the news.

Because we live in a culture in which many people are encouraged to do "whatever it takes" to claw their way to the top, some don't think twice about lying to make a point, taking ethical shortcuts or stretching the truth. In fact, these types of dishonesty are so common, you may be saying, "That's no big deal. Everybody does that stuff."

Yet, this kind of "stuff" chips away at your personal integrity and influences others to justify the same minor lies. Most people do not make a conscious decision to sacrifice their integrity by making one big, bad mistake. Instead, bad choices — all of which seem minor at the time — accumulate. One bad choice leads to another. *That's* how most people lose their integrity — one minor infraction of dishonesty at a time.

The line between small lies and big lies is invisible because it doesn't exist. The fact is, once you start making excuses, they become a little easier each time. Soon, you find yourself in a place you never envisioned you would be. You may have *thought* you knew the difference between a small lie and a big one, but …

Sin begets sin. It will take you farther than you planned to go, remain with you longer than you planned for it to stay and cost you more than you planned to pay.

Just as the line between a small and large lie is nonexistent, neither does integrity come in varying degrees. A little bit of integrity is not possible. It is all-inclusive. You cannot pick and choose when to be a person of integrity. You either are … or you aren't.

A person of integrity lasts. The Bible says: "*Blessed is the man who perseveres under trial, because when he has stood the test, he will receive the crown of life that God has promised to those that love him.*"[2] And, "*the man of integrity walks securely, but he who takes crooked paths will be found out.*"[3] Think about that: He who takes crooked paths will be found out, but a man of integrity walks securely.

The integrity gap

A huge gap exists between the world's standard for integrity and God's standard. You can't straddle the integrity gap and jump to whichever side is the most convenient at the time. You have to choose your side and stick with it.

On one side, you have the world's standard of integrity: Don't get caught.

On the other side is God's standard. Do what is right — regardless of the consequences — and resemble the conduct of Jesus Christ. Paul wrote, "*Do not be overcome by evil, but overcome evil with good.*"[4] There is no gray area. David spoke of integrity protecting him. He wrote, "*May integrity and uprightness protect me, because my hope is in you.*"[5]

Overcome evil with good, and your integrity protects you.

Psalm 15 defines integrity and explains the results of living a life of integrity: "*Lord, who may dwell in your sanctuary? Who may live on your holy hill? He whose walk is* ***blameless*** *and who does what is* ***righteous****, who speaks the* ***truth*** *from his heart and has* ***no slander*** *on his tongue, who does his neighbor* ***no wrong*** *and casts* ***no slur*** *on his fellowman, who despises a vile man but* ***honors those who fear the Lord****, who* ***keeps his oath*** *even when it hurts, who* ***lends his money*** *without usury and* ***does not accept a bribe*** *against the innocent. He who does these things will never be shaken.*"

Imagine the pleasure of working with and around people who fit this description. A blameless, righteous, truthful person who always keeps promises and who always does the right thing — even when it hurts — is the type of person you want to be, and the type of person you want to be around.

Live with integrity, and you will never be shaken.

Integrity Power

Visualize yourself as an iceberg in the ocean. People see what peers above the water — your image and personality. Unseen, below the water level, is the much larger, greater and more powerful foundation — your character and integrity.

Many people spend more time polishing their image than establishing and protecting their integrity; they are more concerned with how they look or sound than with what they do. Ultimately, people will judge one another based on character and integrity, not image. And today, the speed of sharing information makes it possible to see below the waterline much faster than ever before.

Eventually your integrity will be exposed. Before your integrity test, you must decide which side of the integrity gap you will stand.

How to Guard Your Integrity

Because integrity is so important, what can you do to guard it like you would your most precious possession? Four key areas will define your integrity.

1. Do what you say you will do.

It may sound simple, but a mistake many people make is over-committing or committing to something beyond their control. The Bible says: "*It is better to say nothing than to make a promise and not keep it. Don't let your mouth make you sin.*"[6] Living up to your commitments is one of the principal ways people judge your integrity. The ultimate test of your integrity is whether you do what you say you will do.

People judge your word and your commitment every time you say you are going to do something — regardless of how insignificant you consider the commitment. Simply stated, "*Let your yes be yes, let your no be no.*"[7] People hear what you say and watch how you deliver the message, but they react to what they see you do. You can't fake integrity. Do what you say you will do.

If things change …
Unexpected events happen and a time may come when you cannot keep your word. A situation may change, new information may surface, or your stance may change and you cannot do what you said. It happens to everyone occasionally. When that happens, communicate the reason thoroughly, honestly and quickly to minimize the damage.

Don't be like Herod who made a promise and refused to change because of his ego: "*When the daughter of Herodias came in and danced, she pleased Herod and his dinner guests. The king said to the girl, 'Ask me for anything you want, and I'll give it to you.' And he promised her with an oath, 'Whatever you ask I will give you, up to half my kingdom.' She went out and said to her mother, 'What shall I ask for?' 'The head of John the Baptist,' she answered.*"[8]

And Herod delivered it to her.

Herod was upset that he made the promise but went ahead and kept his oath because he did not want to look bad in front of his dinner guests. When you make a mistake, don't make it worse by keeping a promise just to save yourself from looking bad. Acknowledge that things changed, or that you should not have made the promise, or that you did not have the authority to keep your promise. Be honest and be sensible!

2. Stand up and speak out for what you believe.
Do you know exactly what you believe? What is so important in your life that you never will compromise it for any reason? The Bible says to "*always be prepared to give an answer to everyone who asks you to give the reason for the hope that you have.*"[9] Don't leave people guessing about how you feel or where you stand.

People are watching you. You influence the thoughts and behaviors of people around you — perhaps much more than you think. You have no choice about being a role model for others. The only choice you *do* have is which role you will model.

After the 1996 football season, Heisman trophy winner Danny Wuerffel shocked the sports world by declining an invitation to be named Playboy's National Scholar Athlete of the Year. Why decline the award?

"It didn't take any thought at all," Wuerffel said. "It would've been a lot of fun, and I'm sure there's a good bit of the population out there that would think I'm silly for doing this. But there's also a good bit of the population that would understand that's not the type of person I would want to portray myself as."

Danny Wuerffel had no idea of his influence. One 9-year-old boy, Tim Tebow in Ponte Vedra, Florida, was watching with interest the stance Wuerffel took. Ten years later, Tebow led the Florida Gators to two national championships, and it was his turn to take a stance.

Every Saturday of the football season, Tebow exposed millions of people to a message scripted in the eye black on his face. He displayed Philippians 4:6, John 3:16 and many other scriptures for all to see. People from all over America dusted off their Bibles to search and see what Tebow proclaimed.

Only God knows the impact Tebow had on another 9-year-old — or 30-year-old — kid who watched him. His impact began with Danny Wuerffel's influence; Wuerffel never knew it at the time.

You may never know the difference you make in someone's life. Everything you do counts. What are those around you seeing in you?

3. Restrain your tongue.
"Do you not know that your body is a temple of the Holy Spirit, who is

in you, whom you have received from God? You are not your own; you were bought at a price. Therefore honor God with your body."[10]

Few would argue that you do not honor God when you destroy your body with sexual immorality, alcohol, nicotine or other drugs. The challenge is to take care of all of your body … including the tongue. In the Old Testament, we learn, "*Those who control their tongue will have a long life; opening your mouth can ruin everything.*"[11]

You are to keep your whole body in check, including your tongue.

James provided the following illustration:[12] "*When we put bits into the mouths of horses to make them obey us, we can turn the whole animal. Or take ships as an example. Although they are so large and are driven by strong winds, they are steered by a very small rudder wherever the pilot wants to go. Likewise the tongue is a small part of the body, but it makes great boasts. Consider what a great forest is set on fire by a small spark. The tongue also is a fire, a world of evil among the parts of the body. It corrupts the whole person, sets the whole course of his life on fire, and is itself set on fire by hell. All kinds of animals, birds, reptiles and creatures of the sea are being tamed and have been tamed by man, but no man can tame the tongue. It is a restless evil, full of deadly poison.*"

Controlling the tongue is a fulltime job; it is a restless evil full of deadly poison. Your tongue should be used to glorify God and encourage others — not as a weapon to insult, criticize, speak scandalous whispers, gossip or contradict your values.

Two basic questions to ask yourself before speaking are: Is it true? And, is it necessary that I share this information? "*Do not let unwholesome talk come out of your mouths, but only what is helpful for building others up according to their areas, that it may benefit those who listen.*"[13]

If your words are true and necessary to share, speak them with confidence. If not, it may be best not to say everything you have heard. Your integrity is at stake.

The Bible says: "*Truthful lips endure forever, but a lying tongue lasts only a moment,*"[14] and "*the Lord detests lying lips but he delights in men who are truthful.*"[15]

So, a lying tongue is detested and temporary. Truth is forever and delights the Lord. You choose.

4. Ask yourself: What is the right thing to do?

Paul instructed Titus not to even put himself in a position where his integrity could be questioned: "*In everything set them an example by doing what is good. In your teaching show integrity, seriousness and soundness of speech that cannot be condemned,* **so that those who oppose you may be ashamed** *because they have nothing bad to say about us.*"[16]

When I was growing up, my parents taught me that the worst thing I could ever lose was my reputation. In our house, we never had to define integrity; we just had to define what we thought was right. In fact, every time I brought an issue to my dad, the first question he would ask me was, "What do you think is the right thing to do?"

Almost every time, I already knew the right thing to do. I was searching for an opening to justify what I wanted to do. I hated my dad's question at the time but upon many years of reflection, I have come to realize that answering the question clarified and cemented the action I needed to take.

My early experiences taught me that if I consistently behaved according to "right" and moral behavior, I could live without shame, without regret and with confidence. To never be ashamed of my reflection became my personal definition of — and measuring stick for — integrity. I knew if I could trust myself, others could trust me, as well.

Rare breed

People who have integrity possess one of the most respected virtues in all of life. In one survey, when asked which trait — in a list of 16 — has the single greatest impact on an executive's effectiveness, 71 percent of 2,300 executives surveyed listed integrity at the top.[17] Think about how difficult it is to get 71 percent of senior executives to agree on anything — especially with 15 other choices.

The participants from that study know the same thing you and I do: If a person sacrifices his integrity, nothing else really matters.

The Bible says, "*Even if you should suffer for what is right, you are blessed.*"[18] What is the right thing to do? Answer that question, and everything else has a good chance of falling into place.

Recovery after an integrity breach

You may have breached your integrity somewhere along the way. It is not too late to recover and reestablish your integrity. No one is perfect and because of our imperfections, Jesus died for us. He will forgive.

Even David — *a man after God's own heart* — allowed himself to get into a major integrity breach with Bathsheba. He committed adultery, ordered a murder, orchestrated a cover-up and involved others in his scandal.[19]

David eventually repented to the Lord and during that time wrote: "*Have mercy on me, O God, according to your unfailing love; according to your great compassion blot out my transgressions. Wash away all my iniquity and cleanse me from my sin.*"[20]

Read the entire chapter of Psalm 51, and you will find the path to recovery from an integrity breach of great magnitude. David was able to recover; you can recover, too.

Summary

Establishing and living a life with integrity is a full-time job. Just one bad experience can counter a lifetime of great service. You have to guard your integrity every day.

Here is how you can live with integrity:

- ✦ Establish integrity as a top priority — the cornerstone of your actions and decisions.
- ✦ Establish crystal-clear values, and communicate them without hesitation.
- ✦ Do what is right, regardless — no hidden agendas, no games, no regrets.
- ✦ Never rationalize a situation as "an isolated incident." There are no isolated incidents.
- ✦ Do what you say you will do.
- ✦ Restrain your tongue
- ✦ Continually ask yourself: "What is the right thing to do?"

Without integrity, you can't develop trust. Without trust, nothing else really matters. Guard your integrity like it's your most prized possession, because that's exactly what it is.

Questions for Discussion

- ✦ Describe a person in your life who exhibits unwavering integrity.
- ✦ Is there anyone in your life you deeply admired who disappointed you with an integrity breach? Were there any indications the breach would happen? How did you feel? Did he recover?
- ✦ Name three integrity breaches that you perceive "everyone does."
- ✦ Recall a situation where someone you know went against the tide publicly that helped you confirm your own stance on an issue.
- ✦ Discuss the following terms and reflect on the damage the tongue can deliver: Lie, perjury, rash judgment, detraction, flattery, adulation, boasting.

chapter 3

Prioritize Your Priorities

"I have come that they may have life, and have it to the full."
– JOHN 10:10

Prioritizing your priorities.

That is a challenge you will face in every quarter of your life. Important things compete for your time and energy. No matter how much "success" you have, if your priorities are out of sync with your values, you will never be happy.

Prioritizing priorities can feel overwhelming at times. Many things come at you from different directions, making it difficult to separate the important from the trivial. It is like playing a never-ending game of Whack-a-Mole. As soon as you knock one "crisis" down, another pops up.

Your ability to navigate through priorities in the right order is key to living life to the fullest, regardless of which quarter you are living.

All kinds of tricks

Many of Aesop's fables teach modern-day lessons. One of my favorite lessons comes from the fable, "The Fox and the Cat." Here is the story:

> A fox boasted to a cat one day about how sly and wily he was.
>
> "I've got all kinds of tricks," the fox said. "For example, whenever I hear the dogs coming, I know a hundred different ways to escape."
>
> The cat was impressed and humbly said, "Your cleverness is amazing. As for me, I have only one way to escape, and that is to climb up a tree. I know it's not as exciting as all of your ways, but it works for me. Maybe someday you could show me some of your different escape routes."
>
> The fox smiled smugly, "Well, friend, perhaps I'll have some free time one of these days, and I can show you a trick or two."
>
> Shortly afterward, the fox and the cat heard a pack of hounds baying nearby.
>
> "They're coming this way!" the cat shrieked. In a flash, she scaled a nearby tree and hid herself in the leaves. The fox stood there trying to decide which of his many tricks to use. Paralyzed with indecision, the fox waited too long to make his move, and the hounds pounced on him.

The moral of the story: Having too many choices can lead to indecision and inaction. Just like the fox, when you have too many "main" things going on, you become paralyzed and take no action at all.

If everything is a priority, you do not have any priority. You have to learn to keep the main thing the main thing. Everything cannot be your main thing. Confusion about what is really important will create chaos in your quest to have a balanced life.

Who do you want to become

Live life to the fullest. What does that truly mean? Living life to the fullest requires simplifying life by answering — definitively, without a doubt, unequivocally — "Who do I want to become?" Then, spend your time, efforts and resources becoming that person.

But before you answer the question, "Who do I want to become?" look around. If you are like most, you will become very similar to the five people that you spend the most time with. Those five people probably reflect who you are in the process of becoming. They could be a blessing, or they could be a barrier preventing you from living your life to the fullest.

Focus

Becoming the person you want to be requires laser-sharp focus. With a crystal clear answer of "Who do I want to become," priorities will prioritize themselves, and you can begin living life to the fullest. You have pointed your laser directly at your most important priority.

Certainly, many external factors compete for your focus. Life is complex. And the more complicated things are, the easier it is to lose focus. Even back in the early part of the 20th century, Henry Ford believed all human beings tried to do too many things at once.

"That scatters effort and destroys direction," he said. "Every now and then I wake up in the morning with a dozen things I want to do. I know I can't do them all at once."

When asked what he did about that, Ford replied, "I go out and trot around the house. While I'm running off the excess energy that wants to do too much, my mind clears, and I see what can be done and should be done first."

Clarity — that's where knowing "who do I want to become" comes into play. All too often, *you* become the source of complexity and instability, rather than a source of simplicity and stability. Spending time on things that do not lead you toward the person you want to be is choosing to do something less important.

Take a minute — right now — and write on paper or your computer a one-paragraph description of whom you want to become. It does not have to be a perfectly crafted paragraph. Just start writing down character traits you want. Your answer may change as you work your way through this book.

Once you establish who you want to become, master two areas to organize your life and stay on the right track: Elimination of clutter and connecting with the right people. Mastering these tasks help create order in life.

Unclutter

Clutter fills your days. You can spend every hour of every day sorting through the clutter of news, information, social media and other "things" that pop up unintentionally each day. Think about it: Do most of those things that clutter your time and attention help you become the person you want to be? Maybe not.

Is uncluttering a new challenge? The source of your clutter may be new, but maintaining focus and eliminating clutter has been around since the beginning of time. Even Paul taught about uncluttering when he wrote to the church of Ephesus, "*Be very careful, then, how you live – not as unwise but as wise, making the most of every opportunity…*"[1]

To the Corinthian church he taught that, "*everything should be done in a fitting and orderly way.*"[2] Clearing out the clutter means making the most of every opportunity and doing everything in a fitting and orderly way.

One common denominator of successful people is being extremely organized. They have time for their family, enjoy hobbies that help them reboot, attend church to kindle their spiritual fire and live life to the fullest. They are uncluttering experts. They know the people they want to be and prioritize their lives to become those people.

Managing your attention

So, how can you unclutter? Is there a magic formula? How do you take control of your time and your life?

You may have been told growing up, perhaps after turning in a term paper three days late, to learn to manage your time better. No kidding. How do you manage time? *Time* is not manageable. No matter what you do, time marches on — tick, tick, tick — and nothing you do can change that.

In fact, time is a great equalizer; it runs at the same speed for everybody, rich or poor, jet pilot or snail farmer. Time *seems* to run faster when you're out with friends, but slower when you're sitting in the doctor's waiting room. However, it's still chugging along at its normal pace — exactly 168 hours a week — leaving behind a trail of unrecoverable seconds and minutes and hours.

What you do manage, though, is your attention.

Attention is a resource we all possess. It's a lot like time. In fact, as long as we are awake, we produce a continuous stream of attention. But how effectively do you use this valuable resource? That depends on where you direct your attention and how intensely you stay focused on the goal of becoming the person you want to be.

Your attention reflects your conscious decisions about which activities will occupy your time. The world we live in today is connected as never before. You are LinkedIn, Facebooked, Twittered, mapped, GPS'd, Web Paged, My Spaced, emailed, blogged, IM'd,

Yahooed and Googled with real-time news alerts, stock updates and traffic reports.

Earth-orbiting satellites know where you are every second, how many inches you are from your favorite restaurant and whether your air bags have deployed. You can be so connected you forget where your attention should be.

So, how can you maintain focus, clear out clutter, make more room for Christ and become the person that you want to be?

You have to take control of your attention to take control of your life. Here are 10 organizational tips to help decrease the clutter in your life so you can spend more attention on becoming the person you want to be.[3]

1. **Own your day.**
   Granted, some minutes and hours may already be absorbed by meetings, phone calls, commute times, etc. However, you still control most of the hours in the day. Own that time, and make better decisions for the time of which you have total control.

   Don't make excuses about time; everybody has the same amount. Own your day.

2. **Do you know where your time goes?**
   Clutter results from not taking the time to clean up the mess. Keep track of how you spend your time for two weeks. OK, you may not want to do it for two weeks, but how about two days?

   You may be thinking you do not have the time to track everything you do. That is the point! Think of tracking your time like a calorie counter. It is annoying but enlightening. The results will show you where you invest your attention and where your time is "cluttered" up.

Without tracking your time, you will not know what to change. Once you understand the reality of where you spend your time, you can make better decisions and begin to unclutter your life.

3. **Attack procrastination.**
   It's a nasty habit that costs a lot of time, energy and frustration.

   Putting things off seldom improves the quality of your work. In fact, knowing you have something to do that already should have been done only increases stress.

   The best time management question of all time is, "What is the best use of my time *right now*?" Don't procrastinate. Instead, make the best use of your time.

4. **Do one important thing at a time.**
   What about multitasking? For most people, multitasking messes everything up simultaneously; it's a great way to do nothing well in a hurry. Granted, if you are multitasking trivial things, you can knock out two trivial things at once.

   However, if you attempt to multitask important things, you only ask for trouble. You will find yourself switching between things you should be doing and things you shouldn't be doing. Important things require dedicated focus.

5. **Master specificity.**
   Be specific about what you ask from someone. Answer the basics, such as who, what, when and where.

   Take control of even the small things. For instance, when someone says to you, "Call me later, and we'll set an appointment," respond by saying, "Lets save ourselves a call and make the appointment now." Then it's done … and you won't have to spend another 15 minutes on a phone call just to arrange a meeting.

6. **Throw things away.**
   Ask yourself, "What is the worst thing that could happen if I throw this away?" Most of the time, you can live with the answer, so start filling your wastebasket. What about electronic communications? Every computer has a delete button. Make it your friend.

7. **Perfection paralysis is expensive.**
   Sometimes, making things "perfect" is not worth the effort. Take a look at time costs involved, and weigh them against the benefit of perfection. Avoid spending more time on things that simply don't require it.

   If you are like most, you will not get much of anything done unless you go ahead and do something before the timing is completely perfect.

8. **Time chunk.**
   Bundle similar activities together to avoid frequent starting and stopping. For example, listen to all your voicemails at once. Return all emails and phone calls at one time. Write all correspondence in one sitting. Eliminate as many transitions from one activity to another as possible.

9. **Accept that you will never be able to please everyone.**
   Always be candid, and learn to say "no" to things you do not need to commit. Thinking you can wave a magic wand and please everyone — including your closest family members — is fooling yourself. Being honest upfront will save you time and frustration in the long haul.

10. **Reflect and review.**
    Follow Ben Franklin's advice. Begin your day asking yourself, "What good shall I do this day?" End your day answering, "What good have I done today?"

One last tip on clutter: Beware of social media. If you are like most, it absorbs your attention, and you may not even know it. Social media covers the gamut; it's a great way to keep in touch with friends, but also a great way to waste a whole lot of time.

You have to decide whether it is worthwhile to you. Just be aware: The use of energy and emotions generated by social media may prevent you from becoming the person you want to be.

Connect

Prioritizing your priorities and living life to the fullest requires connecting to other people who can help you become the person you want to become.

Since Adam whispered his first words to Eve, people have been attempting to connect. Billions of words are spoken every day. But, connecting isn't just about talking. It's about filling one of the deepest needs of all people — the desire to be understood.

Family counselors will confirm that communication is a missing ingredient in broken homes. Schoolteachers will verify that communication skills are essential to social acceptance, even in pre-school. Within organizations, the issue most often voiced is, "Our organization does not communicate." How many times have your children said to you, "But you didn't tell me?"

Actually, communication may not be the problem, and communicating more may not be the solution. In most cases, people do not need more information. Instead, most information they receive doesn't get attention; that which gets read is frequently misunderstood; and that which is understood usually is not remembered.

So, communicating more will probably not help; *connecting* more will.

Your ability to connect with people is one requirement of success in all areas of your life. All people need to be connected. However, no matter how much you text, voicemail, e-mail or speak, nothing replaces personal connections.

There is a time and place for all those other methods of communication, but don't allow them to replace your personal touch.

How to Connect

The Bible illustrates several ways to connect with people.

Through a fire in a bush, God connected with Moses about becoming the leader of his people. In this instance, the power of God's communication was **using the unexpected** to get Moses' attention.

Paul communicated passionately. Before his conversion, he passionately persecuted Christians. After his conversion experience, Paul communicated the good news of Jesus with the same **sincerity and passion**. He was a great connector because of his passion about what he communicated. He could not hide his passion and commitment.

Barnabas connected through **encouragement**. He risked his life encouraging Paul when others were skeptical of Paul's conversion. By encouraging Paul and Mark, Barnabas had a direct and positive influence on the early Christian movement.

Examine how Jesus connected with people:

- ✦ He chose to connect through parables, often multiple parables with the same meaning. He knew that people could **relate to the experiences** of other people.
- ✦ He was a consistent, faithful listener. He made connecting with his Heavenly Father a priority and acted upon the direction

discovered through his prayers. He was a **great listener**, a requirement for effective connection.

- ✦ He connected by **touching people**. He went to people in order to touch them, be with them, provide direction and empathize with their needs. He communicated to them according to their individual comfort levels — whether peasant or king.

Connecting is individualized. Some of the biblical connecting tools include encouragement, touch, listening, sincerity, passion and connecting through an unexpected form of communication. All of them depended on the experiences of the people needing connection.

Compassionate connecting

Whether you consciously hear it or not, those around you are asking the question, "Do you really care?" The most effective way to demonstrate you care is to invest your time with them. Becoming who you want to be requires you to bring others on the trip with you. If they are convinced that you don't care about them, don't expect them to come along just for the ride.

Even with Jesus, He was asked, "Don't you care?" at least twice in his ministry.

The disciples, who had seen many of His miracles in person, questioned Him when they felt afraid and perceived danger. When they were in their boat during a storm, they woke Jesus with the question, "*Teacher, don't you care?*"[4]

Can you imagine? Even after all the miracles they witnessed, they still questioned Jesus.

When Martha felt frustrated because she thought she was being mistreated by having to do her sister's work, she asked, "*Lord, don't you care?*"[5]

Jesus was a master at prioritizing priorities. He knew the trivial versus what was important. He told Martha to take a deep breath, relax and adjust her focus to the one thing that was important.

If Jesus had to answer the question, don't you care, think how much more often we have to answer the same question. When is the last time anyone saw you performing miracles?

Connecting at work

Let's face it; most of us will work almost all of our lives. Most of us will have to work for someone. I am thankful to be able to work, and I think King Solomon had it right when he said, "*It is good and proper to find satisfaction in his toilsome labor, be happy in our work – this is a gift of God.*"[6]

Working is a gift for which we should be grateful.

I have observed that most people do not quit their jobs; they quit work relationships. For example, a relationship at work sours due to miscommunication, unclear expectations, or a misunderstanding. You become disappointed in the person you work for, so you go somewhere else to try another relationship.

Unfortunately, most people will discover the new boss is similar to the old boss. The problem may not be the boss; it may be the *connection* between you and the boss. Whether your boss is great or the relationship is strained, you have the responsibility to facilitate a positive relationship between the two of you.

Few successful people have worked for excellent bosses their entire career. In fact, according to one study,[7] only 14 percent of workers had positive role models. Eighty-six percent of people do not have a positive role model at work. As difficult as it is to accept, somewhere along the way, you will face bosses who do not share your values, who don't provide clear visions and who feel indifferent about creating positive relationships.

Managing relationships at work is a challenge you will encounter in all four quarters of your life. A bad relationship with your boss can throw you off track from becoming the person you want to be. The time to quit may come, but maybe you need to manage the relationship with your boss into a positive arena.

Jesus taught us how to deal with an arrogant boss in the parable of the persistent widow in Luke 18. In that parable, her "boss" neither feared God nor cared about the people. Jesus' direction was simple: "*Always pray and do not give up.*"[8] It is easier to work with people when you pray for them daily. Even when you choose to no longer work for a particular person, never give up your prayers for him.

Upward communication goes against organizational gravity and requires courage. If you make positive connections with your boss a priority, your relationship will improve, and you will become closer to being the person you want to be.

A positive, productive working relationship is important for three reasons. One, your own job satisfaction depends largely on a productive relationship with your boss. Two, your family depends on you to support them, regardless of who happens to be your boss. Third, your relationship is important because the better you connect with your boss, the happier you will be at home.

The time you spend developing a positive relationship with those at work will yield improved performance, and increased job satisfaction for you and your family. Do not leave that relationship to chance; manage the relationship the same way you would manage a relationship with someone who works for you.

If nothing works

The time may come when you have to leave your current situation. You have done all you can — given it your best shot — but nothing works. That is okay if you leave for the right reasons. If you're placed in an unethical, immoral or illegal situation, or if your misery at work is affecting your health, you need to leave quickly. However, if you're not in a crisis, my advice is to never run *away* from a problem. If you leave a job, run *toward* a new opportunity.

I believe that God does not call us away from most problems; he calls us toward new opportunities. If the opportunity is not worth running to, be the very best where you are, and wait until the right opportunity comes along. Then, run toward it.

SUMMARY

A friend once told me that what keeps people from moving forward is not the mountain ahead but the grain of sand in the shoe. That "grain of sand" may be disguised as the clutter of everyday life or important connections that are disconnected.

After you answer definitively, "Who do I want to become," then:

- ✦ Get organized, and eliminate the clutter preventing you from becoming the person you want to be.
- ✦ Connect with the important people who will help you become the person you want to be.
- ✦ Prioritize the priorities in your life.

"But ***seek first his kingdom*** *and his righteousness, and all these things will be given to you as well."*[9]

QUESTIONS FOR DISCUSSION

- ✦ What does "life to the fullest" mean to you?
- ✦ If you haven't done it already, complete your paragraph on, "Who do I want to become?"
- ✦ How do you prioritize your priorities?
- ✦ Which three of the organization tips can you begin doing today?
- ✦ If you were a boss, how would you feel about someone approaching you to clarify his priorities?
- ✦ What is the best way to work through a serious conflict at work?

chapter 4

Take Optimism With You

"Whatsoever things are true, whatsoever things are honest, whatsoever things are just, whatsoever things are pure, whatsoever things are lovely, whatsoever things are of good report, if there be any virtue, and if there be any praise, think on these things."
– PHILIPPIANS 4:8 (KJV)

Preparing for your second quarter involves digging your faith well deep, living with integrity, prioritizing your priorities and living your life with optimistic faith. Optimism and faith go hand-in-hand. It is impossible to be a pessimistic, cynical person who is filled to the brim with faith.

What do you see?

"An optimist sees an opportunity in every calamity; a pessimist sees a calamity in every opportunity." That was Winston Churchill's view. The following story illustrates his point, depicting how optimistic people see the potential others fail to realize:

> A large shoe manufacturer independently dispatched two researchers to one of the world's least developed countries. Their task was to assess the business possibilities within that country.

> The first report came back to the manufacturer's headquarters and read: "No market here. Nobody wears shoes!"
>
> A few days later, the second report came back from the other researcher. It read: "Great market here. Nobody wears shoes!" Same country, same situation, but the researchers each had different outlooks.

If you were to conduct a survey and ask, "Are you an optimistic person," I believe most people would say, "Sure, absolutely. I am optimistic." They probably would add, "but I am a realist."

Even the first guy in the shoe story above would consider himself an optimist but also a realist. Like many people, he fixated on one thing and could not see the greater picture. He was not an optimist or a realist.

An optimist is like the second guy in the story. He looked beyond the obvious and saw something good in the situation; he focused on the opportunity.

Optimism is a state of mind. It results from a person's desire and effort to *choose* to accept every situation and make the best of those situations. Certainly, the road of optimism is not without potholes. Everyone faces unexpected and sometimes destructive setbacks and events. The question is not *will* you face difficult situations; the question is *how* do you move forward, regardless of the situation?

The optimistic Christian exhibits faith by recognizing defeat as a temporary setback — isolated to a given situation. Unexpected events happen. Forced and unfamiliar paths will test your faith. No one enjoys the unknown, but regardless of the struggles you confront, you still can expect the best possible outcome. What you expect ultimately will influence what happens down the road.

Paul reflected: "*I have great confidence in you. I take great pride in you. I am greatly encouraged; in all our troubles my joy knows no bounds.*"[1]

In all our troubles my joy knows no bounds? Is he crazy? Did he really mean in all our successes my joy knows no bounds? I think Paul would say "no matter what," my joy knows no bounds. He trusted God's provision, regardless of success or troubles.

When something happens
"Something can be done, and there is something I can do."

I am not sure exactly where I heard that sentence for the first time. Whoever shared it with me gave me a wonderful gift; it has been a source of comfort and strength throughout my life. Something can be done — whatever hole you are in is not permanent — something can be done right now. And, there is something you can do; you get to make the next move.

Not everything that happens to you is going to be great; you don't live in a Pollyanna world. But, you can react to whatever happens to you in a positive, optimistic manner. The Bible instructs us to, "*give thanks in all circumstances; for this is God's will for you in Christ Jesus.*"[2]

Give thanks in all circumstances. No stipulations. No passes for bad economy, bad bosses, bad luck or poor choices … no stipulations at all. Give thanks in *all* circumstances.

Optimistic people refuse to waste their energy worrying about situations over which they have no control. Author Charles Dickens advised, "Reflect upon your present blessings, of which every man has many — not on your past misfortunes, of which all men have some."

Everyone has misfortunes; everyone has blessings. You have the choice to focus on what will help you become the person you want to be.

Combat the Enemies

Two of optimism's greatest enemies are worry and painful emotions that create anxiety and fear.

The word "worry" is derived from an Anglo Saxon word meaning "to choke or strangle." It is to torment oneself with or suffer from disturbing thoughts. Worry creates fear, drains energy, prevents you from achieving potential, and obstructs you from obtaining goals.

Not much good happens when you are paralyzed with worry.

Most of what people worry about is beyond their control to change anyway. If you are like me, a large portion of what you worry about is what people will think or say about you. You do not have any control over what they think or say.

Why not spend your time doing something they will admire and then let them talk all they want? Or, as Paul said, hush them up, "*so those that oppose you may be ashamed because they have nothing bad to say about us.*"[3]

What you do to prevent the worry is entirely under your control. The antidote to worry is to proactively do something to keep your worry away.

Jesus was explicit in his teachings about worry. He asked, "*Who of you by worrying can add a single hour to his life?*"[4] Later, He said, "*Do not worry about tomorrow, for tomorrow will worry about itself. Each day has enough trouble of its own.*"[5] Jesus knew the negative effects of worry. It torments you.

A famous study[6] estimated the average person worries about:

- ✦ Things that will never happen — 40 percent of the time.
- ✦ Things about the past that can't be changed — 30 percent of the time.

- ✦ Things about criticism by others, mostly untrue — 12 percent of the time.
- ✦ Health, which gets worse with stress — 10 percent of the time.
- ✦ Real problems that can be solved — 8 percent of the time.

Someone once told me that because 40 percent of what we worry about will never happen, worrying must work. That is a pretty clever analysis and proves you can make any case you want to with statistics. However, I believe Corrie ten Boom was right when she said, "Worry does not empty tomorrow of its sorrow. It empties today of its strength."

A person consumed by worry cannot live life to the fullest at home or at work.

Many years ago, Dr. Charles Mayo observed that worry not only puts a strain on our mental health, but on our physical health, too. Since his discovery, researchers have connected chronic worry to weakened immune systems, cardiovascular disease, neurological imbalances, clinical depression and other physical and psychological dysfunctions.

So, those who say they are worried sick or worried to death are probably right.

Consistent worrying is like putting your car in neutral and revving the engine. It burns oil and gas and is hard on the engine; it doesn't get you anywhere, either. Mayo confirmed what Solomon wrote centuries ago: "*An anxious heart weighs a man down but a kind heart cheers him up.*"[7]

Paul taught us not to worry about anything, but to pray about everything: "*Do not be anxious about anything, but in everything, by prayer and petition, with thanksgiving, present your request to God.*"[8]

To worry less, try praying more.

In the parable of the four soils, Jesus taught about those who hear the word of God, but "*as they go their way become choked by life's worries, riches and pleasures, and they do not mature.*"[9]

Think about being choked. Is there anything worse than not being able to take a breath? When you were a kid and had your breath knocked out, was anything more frightening? You were scared almost to death. Don't be choked by life's worries or allow them to consume the energy and optimism you have.

Not worrying isn't easy. For most, including me, it is a real struggle. Everyone has plenty to worry about if we choose: Personal problems, financial issues, concerns about our children and parents, and plenty of other things that pop up. But the fact is, worry cannot change the past, and worry does not have to control our future.

Jesus acknowledged that we do struggle, and He provided for our relief. "*Come to me, all you who are weary and burdened, and I will give you rest. Take my yoke upon you and learn from me, for I am gentle and humble in heart, and you will find rest for your souls. For my yoke is easy and my burden is light.*"[10]

He did not promise us a life without burdens; He provided a way to handle the burdens we carry.

Something can be done …
You can do something about your natural tendency to worry. Try the following:

- **Get the facts.**
  Most worry is based on false assumptions — your assumption about things you fear will happen as opposed to what actually is happening. That means that most of the time you do not own what you are worrying about — you are borrowing your

worry based on an assumption. The worry is not yours. Don't borrow worry. Ask yourself, "Do I own this worry?" If you own it, you have the control to do something about it. If you are borrowing it, you can't fix it so you might as well stop worrying about it. Get the real facts, and try not to dwell on the unknown fears that drain energy.

- **Consider the worst possible outcome.**
  If your worry is among the small percent over which you have control, what will be the effect if it does come to pass? Once you discover the worst possible outcome, you often will find it to not be as bad as you thought. You probably can live with it, even though you may have to make some changes. Your stress normally comes from not understanding the worst possible outcome so you can deal with it.

- **Take action.**
  Create a plan that will begin purposeful action to ensure the worst does not happen. It is difficult to worry about things you are working diligently to improve. The antidote to worry is taking action to prevent your worry from happening.

- **Pray about it, and let it go.**
  A Barna study[11] revealed that only 31 percent of Americans pray daily. That means a lot of people try to carry their burdens alone. We evidently do not live in a "don't worry about anything, pray about everything" society. If you have done everything you can to prevent the worry from happening, have taken steps toward solving the issue, and you have asked for God's help, let it go. Your worrying is not helping anyone or anything. In fact, it probably is making you and those around you miserable.

What about Those Unpleasant Emotions?

A second enemy of optimistic faith is the group of nasty, persistent, unpleasant and pessimistic emotions such as hate, fear, doubt, jealousy, self-pity, anger and resentment. Everyone has painful emotions. Your job is to minimize the damage they can cause.

Many times, your uncomfortable emotions come disguised as discouragement. We all fall into the discouragement hole occasionally. That is normal and expected, but discouragement is not from God. You bring it on yourself.

When you are in that discouragement hole, quit digging and get out as fast as you can. Get out of the hole by encouraging someone else. Do a kind act and then try to be discouraged; you may find that difficult.

The Bible says, "*The Lord himself goes before you and will be with you: he will never leave you nor forsake you. Do not be afraid; do not be discouraged.*"[12]

The Bible also says to "fear not" or "don't be afraid" more than 300 times. Why is this repeated so many times? Probably because fear and discouragement are two of the biggest challenges you have to face and will consume you if you let them.

To combat unpleasant emotions and discouragement, first acknowledge the reality of the emotion. What you feel is real. You experience its effects and negative impact on you. Don't ignore or deny those painful feelings. Do something about it. Solomon observed that there is a time for everything. He went into detail of good times and bad. All of those times will happen to us, but his encouragement at the end of his observations was, "*We cannot fathom what God has done from beginning to end. I know that there is nothing better for men than to be happy and do good while they live.*"[13] It is impossible to be happy and to do good things while you are in a negative, discouraging spiral.

Then, stop beating yourself up or blaming others for your situation.

That creates more negativity and does nothing to solve the problem or make you more effective. Placing blame will not solve the problem or cause the painful feeling to disappear. Blame always focuses on the past and does not do anything to solve your current situation. Don't waste your energy on finding whom to blame.

The faster you can learn to say, "I am responsible for my painful emotion of ________," the quicker you will be productive again. Accepting responsibility forces you to focus on the future so you can begin to turn painful feelings into positive actions.

One last thing about painful emotions, if you have any unfinished business contributing to the painful feelings, go to the person and ask him or her to forgive you. Forgiveness will release the guilt from you and allow you to go forward. If you have confessed your sin to God and asked for His forgiveness, accept His forgiveness and become the positive, optimistic person He wants you to be.

Your Attitude Counts

Successful people insist on reliving and recreating past successes. They find ways to duplicate their successes, even though the situation has changed. Contrarily, other people insist on reliving their past failures and wind up duplicating them. They allow their past to consume the future.

Attitude is a magnet. We attract others who have the same attitudes as we. Consider this story:

> A salesman moved into a new town and met an old-timer as he was leaving the bank.
>
> "I'm new to your town. What are the people like here?" the salesman asked.
>
> "What were the people like in the town you came from?" the old-timer responded.

> "Well, they were glum and negative and always complaining, and their glasses were always half-empty," the salesman replied.
>
> "Hmmm," said the old-timer. "Sounds about like the people who live here."
>
> A few weeks later, another person moved to the same town and met the same old-timer as he was leaving the same bank.
>
> "I'm new to your town. What are the people like here?" the newcomer asked.
>
> "What were the people like in the town you came from?" the old-timer responded.
>
> "Well, they were wonderful. They worked together in the neighborhood, helped each other out, and were always there to support us during tough times. We're going to miss them," the newcomer replied.
>
> "Hmmm," said the old-timer. "I think you will like it here. That sounds about like the people who live here."

The old-timer's message? If you want to be around positive, enthusiastic people who are eager to live life to the fullest, your attitude has to be the same. If the people around you seem to be glum and negative, maybe you should check yourself. You may be glum and negative, too.

Gift of awareness
If you think your life is empty of blessings, look around. Blessings happen to you every day, regardless of your current challenges.

A few years ago, during the Christmas season, a friend gave our family a "Blessing Jar," along with another jar full of small, round stones. We placed the jar and stones in a prominent place in our home. According to the instructions accompanying the gift, we were to place a stone in the jar, and thank God every time we acknowledged a blessing.

We did just that. Some of the blessings were huge — like good reports from the doctor. Some were smaller — like I made three birdies playing golf that day.

Suddenly, the jar began filling up. We did not even have to look for blessings to put into our jar; they were obvious to us and coming from every direction. We had to buy more stones and eventually another Blessing Jar.

We told friends, and they would put a stone in our jar and say a blessing. The next Christmas, guess what our "go to" Christmas gift was? Yep, Blessing Jars for all.

The jar was beautiful and thoughtful, but the real gift we received was the gift of awareness. We began to recognize blessings all around us that we previously had overlooked or taken for granted.

Try a "Blessing Jar" with your family. It does not matter the type of jar or stone you use. What *does matter* is the second you take to thank God for His blessing. The old gospel hymn reminds us: "Count your many blessings, name them one by one. Count your many blessings see what God has done."

Look around. Blessings are there for your count if you pay attention.

Look inside

Taking optimism with you requires you to continually look for the best in yourself. Many times, being positive about yourself goes against your nature. You are the most critical of yourself. You probably are far more careful of what you say to others than what you say to yourself. Instead, talk to yourself just like your best friends would talk to you; they would be encouraging, helpful, kind and positive. Many times, your self-talk is just the opposite.

Should we feel that way about ourselves? Of course not! You are one of God's children. "*I praise you because I am fearfully and **wonderfully made**; your works are wonderful, I know that full well.*"[14] You are wonderfully made. The faster you accept that fact, the sooner you will be able to enjoy what God has waiting for you.

It is hard to be positive without letting go of what makes you negative. Even when you feel stressed to the max, you can be a champion at positive self-talk. Replace "I can't" with "I can," "I won't" with "I will," and "we don't" with "we do." It will make a difference in how you feel about yourself and in your ability to carry optimism wherever you go.

Summary

Pessimistic faith. Is that possible? I don't think so. You are supposed to be a resurrected person! You have to choose to be optimistic or pessimistic, to have faith or not. The choices are not interchangeable. Choose to be an optimistic, faithful person instead of a pessimistic person without faith.

Even the most liberal psychologists will confirm that there are few things better for your soul than to be thankful and to have hope for the future.

Here is Paul's advice on how to have optimistic faith:

1. **Don't dwell on your mistakes.** If you have confessed it, accept God's forgiveness. Let your mistake go, and move forward. "*Forgetting what is behind and straining toward what is ahead, I press heavenward in Christ Jesus.*"[15]

2. **Think positive.** You are God's child; act like it. "*I can do everything through Him that gives me strength.*"[16]

3. **Throw away fear.** Fear is tormenting; faith is trusting. The two cannot reside together. "*For God does not give us a spirit of timidity, but a spirit of power, of love, and of self discipline.*"[17]

4. **Keep the dream alive.** Don't abandon your aspirations. "*I want to know Christ, and the power of his resurrection and the fellowship of sharing in his sufferings, becoming like him in his death.*"[18]

In every situation, something can be done and there is something that you can do!

You never will achieve happiness and the ability to remain optimistic by coveting what you perceive others to have. You control your outlook based on your ability to be thankful for your own situation — whatever it might be.

God can be trusted. He loves you and does not want you to live in fear and anxiety. He wants you to feel good while you live! That is the core of how you can be optimistic, regardless of what is going on around you. If you continually pray these words: "Jesus, I trust in you. In all times, I trust in you," your fear and anxiety will subside as you learn to live life to the fullest.

Questions for Discussion

- ✦ Can you have faith and still be pessimistic and cynical?
- ✦ Is there a time when nothing can be done, and you can do nothing?
- ✦ What would Jesus say to the person who dwells on the few negative things that happen in life and ignores the positive happening at the same time?

- ✦ How can you become more aware of the blessings you receive every day? How do you get yourself out of a discouragement hole?
- ✦ What can you do to attack an unpleasant, painful emotion in your life, such as anger, resentment or guilt?
- ✦ How would you describe the type of person you want your children to spend time with?

chapter 5

Pray Like There is No Tomorrow

"The prayer of a righteous person is powerful and effective."
– James 5:16

Praying is the greatest privilege you have during all four quarters of your life. For most, during the second quarter is when you either draw closer to God or stray further from Him. Therefore, the best time to develop a deep relationship with God through your prayer life is *before* you are in the bunker and surrounded by the bullets the second quarter brings.

Please, Lord

A man was running late for his important meeting. When he arrived at the meeting place, the parking lot was full. He began to panic. The meeting was really important; he could not be late. In his panic, he prayed, "Lord, please help me find a parking space."

At the same time he prayed, he saw a parking space become available. Immediately he said, "Never mind, Lord. I just found one."

I love that story. Its subtle points make the story real. First, he talked to God. That is a good thing. He had a relationship and didn't think his issue was too minor to bother God. Second, he did not approach God until he felt panicked. That is not a good thing. Maybe it was just a coincidence, but approaching God should not begin when we feel panicked and begging, "please, Lord."

Third, he gave himself the credit when God answered his prayer. Okay, I got what I asked for, so never mind, Lord. That's not good, either. It might not be unusual for God to answer your prayer, yet you fail to acknowledge God's provision.

Prayer is a personal relationship

The most important relationship you can have is with your Heavenly Father. That relationship is the lynchpin for you to become who you want to be. It is more important than your relationship with your spouse, parent, children, friends or work associates.

Every relationship in your life will improve if you have a consistent, healthy, positive prayer relationship with God. Your relationship with God, through consistent prayer, is priority No. 1. He needs to be involved in every thought, meeting, dinner, commute, worry and victory.

He is available, and His door always stands wide for you to enter.

Mother Teresa of Calcutta may have said it best, "Jesus loves you, but even more — he longs for you. He misses you when you don't come close. He thirsts for you. He loves you always, even when you don't feel worthy."

When you disconnect from God, you lose your spiritual compass. You subject yourself to making decisions you do not want to make. To live life to the fullest, make God your first responder, not your last resort. An active prayer life will change you; you will emerge from prayer different from when you began praying. Prayer and time with Jesus is the priority to prioritize first.

Developing the relationship

Most people feel a little uncomfortable praying. As with any relationship, it takes time and effort to develop. Even the disciples felt uncomfortable praying but were not too proud to ask Jesus for advice. "*One day Jesus was praying in a certain place. When he finished, one of his disciples said to him, Lord, teach us to pray, just as John taught his disciples.*"[1]

Jesus didn't scold them or make them feel foolish; He gave them a prayer. He said to them, "*When you pray, say: 'Father, hallowed be your name, your kingdom come. Give us each day our daily bread. Forgive us our sins, for we also forgive everyone who sins against us. And lead us not into temptation.*'"[2]

He taught them the same prayer he had taught hundreds of people in His sermon on the mount.[3] The prayer Jesus taught His disciples was simple, personal, loving and focused on forgiveness.

A lot of times, I don't know what to pray. My "prayer blockage" might be during a crisis, grief, celebrations or fear. It appears during ordinary times and strange times. The blockage is unpredictable. Regardless of what is going on in your life, you are directed: "*Be joyful in hope, patient in affliction, faithful in prayer.*"[4]

During a prayer blockage, I have found that saying the Lord's Prayer helps me move forward. Also, the words of some of the great hymns I learned as a young kid help me. And, looking around and giving thanks always gets me going.

Should you get hung up on the words? The words we say do not matter most. One of the shortest prayers ever recorded changed one man's life forever.

One of the two thieves hanging on the cross next to Jesus spent his last breath praying: "*Jesus, remember me when you come into your kingdom.*"[5]

That simple, direct request changed his life for eternity. Jesus responded, "*I tell you the truth, today you will be with me in paradise.*"[6]

Sometimes a simple "Jesus, remember me," or a plea of "God, help me," will help you through your own tough times.

Your prayer priority

Consistency is required for great relationships. You want to be with those you love as much as possible. It is important to find a consistent place to connect with Jesus every day. It may be in your favorite chair or on a bench. At daybreak or noon. It could be 10 minutes or 30 minutes on any given day.

The time of day, place of meeting or time spent praying is not as important as the consistency of the meeting. Every day. However long it takes.

Even if you consistently attend church — regardless of how good the sermon or homily — you need more spiritual food than that during the week. To get the most out of your church attendance on Sunday, you need to get the most from your prayer life the other six days. The more you pray and read the Bible, the better you will understand Jesus. You get to know those with whom you spend time. Spend time with Jesus every day, and develop your relationship with Him.

My wife and I have our special time and place together with God. We meet on the porch in good weather, or in my office in bad weather. We spend 10 minutes some days, 30 minutes other days. Our routine is that she will pray, and I then read the scripture for the day. We discuss the scripture and talk about things going on in our lives that need our attention. Then, I close in prayer.

It is nothing fancy, but you would be surprised by how powerful beginning your day with God will be. Try it.

Here are some prayer tips that may help you develop your relationship with God:

1. **Listen.**

   Prayer is a two-way communication between you and God. The Bible gives this direction: "*Guard your steps when you go to the house of God. Go near to listen rather than to offer the sacrifice of fools, who do not know that they do wrong. Do not be quick with your mouth, do not be hasty in your heart to utter anything before God. God is in heaven and you are on earth, so let your words be few.*"[7]

   Take time to listen to God's path for you. "*Be still and know that I am God.*"[8] "*In quietness and trust is your strength.*"[9]

   Create dedicated time to pray and listen to God's direction.

2. **Pray with your Bible open.**

   Your connection and direction from God comes from an intimate prayer life and your consistent study of the Word. Without knowing what is in the word, you can't draw strength from it. Paul advises: "*Faith comes from hearing the message, and the message is heard through the word of Christ.*"[10]

   James takes it one step further and says we must do what the Word says: "*Do not merely listen to the word, and so deceive yourselves. Do what it says. Anyone who listens to the word but does not do what it says is like someone who looks at his face in a mirror and, after looking at himself, goes away and immediately forgets what he looks like.*"[11]

   Paul told Timothy that the Bible is God-breathed and our source of guidance for how to live life to the fullest. "*All Scripture is God-*

breathed and is useful for teaching, rebuking, correcting and training in righteousness, so that the servant of God may be thoroughly equipped for every good work."[12]

Several stories appear in the Bible in which no one recognized Jesus until he spoke. He revealed himself through his words. He does that today; He reveals himself through the Word. Our relationship with Jesus begins with His Word. Every problem you face now, have faced or will face has been addressed in the Bible.

The words written in the Bible are Jesus' gift to you. They equip you to become the person you want to be. Do not let dust settle on your Bible.

3. **Pray whenever, wherever and with whomever.**
   The Bible says, "*Do not put out the Spirit's fire.*"[13] It also directs us to "*pray continually.*"[14]

   Keep the fire burning through a constant connection with God through your ongoing prayer life. Ask the Holy Spirit for guidance in your prayer to lead you to the truth. You do not have to be in a church or chapel. You do not have to close your eyes or kneel. Pray the same way you would talk to your best friend.

4. **Be specific.**
   If you are not specific, how will you know if your prayer is being answered? When the blind beggar asked Jesus to have mercy on him, Jesus asked him, "*What do you want me to do for you?*" Jesus knew what the man wanted, but only after he specifically said, "*Lord, I want to see,*"[15] did Jesus restore his sight. Be specific.

5. ***Give thanks in all circumstances, for this is God's will for you in Christ Jesus.***[16]
   Just like in the story to begin this chapter, sometimes we take God for granted — even when He answers our prayers just the

way we asked. When Jesus healed 10 lepers, only one of the 10 came back and thanked Him.[17] Only one. The other nine focused on the gift, only one focused on the giver. Don't take the giver for granted.

Be thankful when God listens to you and answers your prayers, even when you may not understand His answer.

God, are you there?

Active faith requires active prayer so you can understand God's direction for your life. Sometimes you may convince yourself that your prayers do nothing. Why is God not listening?

God is listening to your prayers — each and every one of them.

Sometimes you may lose your patience while waiting on God's answers. After all, if it was not important and you didn't need an answer, you would not have prayed, right? Maybe He did answer, just in another way than you expected. Maybe the answer is just to continue to do what you are doing. Or, maybe the timing is not right for an immediate answer.

I received one of the greatest gifts of my life on an ordinary Sunday in Houston, Texas, when Dr. John Bisagno preached a sermon on how God answers prayers. His words helped me to understand God's response to my prayers and have been an inspiration to me for more than 30 years. According to Dr. Bisagno, God answers prayer in one of four ways:

- ***Slow.*** The timing is not right. You may have prepared all of your life for an opportunity and think you are ready.

  However, from God's perspective, the timing is not right for you. It may be that the situation is completely different than you think, and it would be a disaster for you to have your prayer answered yes at that particular time.

For whatever reason, the timing is not right for you to get what you ask. I have experienced many prayers answered yes long after I was convinced God had said no. He had answered "not yet."

I may be the most impatient person in the world – for sure in the top five. It is hard for me to, "*Be still and wait on the Lord.*"[18] God has protected me many times by answering my prayers slow. My human nature is to always go. I have to depend on spiritual advisors to help me discern God's answer to my prayers. He has placed specific people in my life at the right time to slow me down and to help me learn how to be still, wait and to prepare for God's perfect timing.

✦ ***Grow*** The timing is right, but *you* are not right. You need to grow before the situation is right for you.

I have witnessed successful people accept a position that led to massive failure. Close friends could see disaster coming … the person's skill sets were not aligned with the job requirements. The pay was more, the office was bigger, the title was impressive, but the job was not right for that particular person at that time. It was a great opportunity for someone else, but a disaster for that person. Sadly, it was obvious to all but the person involved who was swayed by the pay, office and title. God's answer of "no" was reinforced by friends and advisors but he allowed his ego to override God's answer.

Many times, the worst thing that could happen is to get what you pray for. An opportunity might present itself, but that does not mean you are right for that opportunity at that time. In fact, walking into a situation for which you are not prepared could be devastating to you.

You have to trust God's timing. "*Show me your ways, O Lord, teach me your paths, guide me in your truth and teach me, for you are my God and my Savior, and my hope is in you all day long."*[19]

Keep growing, and wait until God opens the right door for you.

- **No.** You — and the timing — are not right. This should be really obvious, but you may panic and try to fit a round peg into a square hole. The timing is not right and you are not right — so pick up and move on. "*Blessed is the man who finds wisdom, the man who gains understanding.*"[20]

  Several years ago, I wrote what I thought would be a best-selling book. It was obvious to me that every publisher would want to participate in bidding to publish my new title, *Monday Morning Leadership*. I prayed that God would give me the wisdom to know which would be the right publisher for me to choose to partner with on this project.

  The manuscript was presented to every major publisher. No one was interested. Not one publishing house made an offer. I could not believe it. My prayer was answered with a definitive "no." There are tens of publishers, and every door was shut. I felt incredibly disappointed.

  The only avenue remaining was to self-publish the book … an expensive and risky route at that time. I chose to try it — a decision that ultimately changed my life. The book sold over a million copies and became the cornerstone of my business.

  Sometimes it is difficult to accept that God closes doors to protect you and allows even better things to happen. That is what happened to me. I prayed diligently for one thing that God answered NO. He provided me something else I would have never had the courage to even ask.

Most of the time, you will not know the reason God answers no until time allows you to look backwards. Then it may be obvious.

✦ ***Go.*** When you and the timing are right, you'll know it. How? You'll have peace. You'll look forward with optimism.

Your trusted advisors will encourage you to move forward. No one has to tell you this opportunity is the right one — you know it. Thank God and enjoy.

You will be like Isaiah when he enthusiastically proclaimed: "*Then I heard the voice of the Lord saying, 'Whom shall I send? And who will go for us?' And I said, 'Here am I. Send me!'*"[21]

Be ready to go when you and the timing are right!

Not always a miracle answer

What happens when God does not answer your prayer the way you prayed and expected? Sometimes He answers your prayers just the way you hoped. Sometimes He answers your prayers in ways better than you would have even asked.

Yet, sometimes He doesn't answer them your way. The Bible says that God is the "*same yesterday and today and forever.*"[22] God's character never changes. However, His ways do change. In the Bible you will see that sometimes He intervenes with a miracle; sometimes He doesn't.

In the book of Acts, Paul and Silas miraculously are released from prison. Later while in prison, Paul was not released and eventually was beheaded in Rome. John the Baptist, who baptized Jesus the Son of God, did not receive a miracle release from prison, and he was beheaded, as well.

When Stephen was seized and imprisoned, he did not receive a miracle release; instead he was stoned to death. In the Old Testament, Moses, Daniel, Jonah and many others miraculously survived when only a miracle would do.

God performed miracles then. God performs miracles today.

Marlea and Elle

I have seen the mystery of prayers answered with a miracle and some answered in ways I will never understand.

Several years ago, my oldest daughter was pregnant with her second child. The pregnancy went as expected and exactly how we had prayed — until it was time for the baby to be born. Then, the unthinkable, unimaginable and horrific happened. Baby Marlea's cord was kinked and wrapped around her neck. She never took a breath on earth.

Nine months of good doctor reports, great expectations … then tragedy. Why did this happen? That is not what we were praying for. No one deserved this. The pain, hurt and sting were beyond comprehension.

About five years later, another daughter of mine was pregnant with her third child. Five months into the pregnancy, the doctors informed my daughter that her baby, Elle, was not going to survive the pregnancy. Her amniotic fluid was low, she was not moving, she had stopped growing, and there was no hope. They instructed my daughter to go home and let nature take its course. Elle's heart was not expected to continue to beat more than a week or so.

Prayers continued for Elle, just like we had prayed for Marlea. My daughter did not go home and wait for Elle to die. She did what was under her control. She put herself on bed rest, drank gallons of water every day, summoned prayer warriors and left Baby Elle's future in God's hands.

Six weeks later, Baby Elle was born weighing in at two pounds, three ounces. After spending several months in the neonatal intensive care unit, she came home from the hospital perfectly healthy.

Our prayers were just as fervent, frequent and sincere for Baby Marlea as they were for Baby Elle. God chose to answer them differently. Marlea's mom handled her situation better than anyone else I know could. She had amazing strength. Elle's mom handled her situation better than anyone else I know. She had amazing strength, too.

I never will understand why those two events happened the way they did. I do know, though, without question, that God's character never changes. Never.

All of my life I had prayed, "Thy will be done." Yet, all along, I probably was praying, "My will be done." Through what appeared to be a tragedy with Marlea and the miracle of Elle, I realized God does not have to conform to our plans or treat each of us the same way. When you say, "Thy will be done," you release yourself from resenting God if He chooses to answer your prayer differently than you wanted Him to answer.

God is not limited in how He answers our prayers; He has all the resources to do what is best for His kingdom and for us. Our job is to trust Him and allow His will to be done in our lives.

When Jesus prayed in the Garden,[23] three times he prayed, "*May this cup be taken from me. Yet not as I will, but as you will.*" Three times he prayed for an easier path than the one before him. God answered His prayer in a way different from what Jesus was praying. God's plan was complete.

If you have made your requests known to God, you have to trust Him even when you do not understand why some things are happening in your life.

Summary

Any day without spending time with the Father is a wasted day. If you feel uncomfortable praying, pray more. There are no instant prayer warriors; you learn to pray by praying. Spending time with God is the antidote to the complexities of life. Your relationship with God creates security and simplification. Your main thing becomes the main thing. Your priorities prioritize themselves.

Prayer is priority one; it is *the* most important relationship you need to cultivate. "*If my people, who are called by my name, will humble themselves and pray and seek my face and turn from their wicked ways, then I will hear from heaven, and I will forgive their sin and will heal their land.*"[24]

God calls you to pray consistently, with an open Bible, and to listen intently for His direction in your life. God is faithful to answer every prayer, but he may not answer with a miracle.

Sometimes, you will not know what to pray. That's okay. The Bible says, "*In the same way, the Spirit helps us in our weakness. We do not know what we ought to pray for, but the Spirit himself intercedes for us through wordless groans.*"[25] It is like you are spending time with a parent. Words do not have to even be uttered; wordless groans are okay. You are there with God.

Pray like there is no tomorrow. "*And pray in the Spirit on all occasions with all kinds of prayers and requests. With this in mind, be alert and always keep on praying for all the Lord's people.*"[26]

Questions for Discussion

- ✦ Do you consider prayer a privilege? Why is it?
- ✦ What should be your goal in prayer?
- ✦ How do you know that you are not just talking to yourself during your prayer time?
- ✦ How has God answered your prayers slow, grow, no or go?
- ✦ Have you prayed for miracles? How was your miracle prayer answered?
- ✦ Has there been a time in your life when what appeared to be a huge disappointment was later discovered to be a blessing?
- ✦ Why does God not answer our prayers the way we think He should?

PART TWO

Prospering During Your Second Quarter

"Consider it pure joy, my brothers,
whenever you face trials of many kinds,
because you know that the testing of your faith
develops perseverance."
– JAMES 1:2-3

chapter 6

Conquer Adversity When it Strikes

"He heals the brokenhearted and binds up their wounds."
– Psalm 147:3

Every person faces adversity. Sometime during life's journey, you will face a life-changing challenge. No one is immune. Adversity is a part of life, a test of your stability, your ability to endure, to continue and to survive. Solomon wrote, *"If you falter in times of trouble, how small is your strength!"*[1]

Nothing reveals your inner strength like adversity does.

Adversity can strike faster than a death adder snake who can go from the strike position, strike and inject venom in its prey, then return back to the strike position all in .15 of a second. The snake strikes so swiftly, victims do not immediately realize they have been bitten. In .15 of a second, lives change forever.

And so it is with adversity. Adversity strikes even the best, most faithful people. Unfortunate things will happen, and you will never understand why. Your faith allows you to cling to your belief that, *"all things work together for the good,"*[2] even in life's darkest hours and when life appears unfair.

Parallel tragedies

Below is a story of adversity and tragedy appearing out of nowhere, striking two loving families who lived hundreds of miles apart:

She was a dynamic businesswoman working for a Fortune 100 company. Armed with a master's degree in business administration from a prestigious university, she usually was the smartest person in any room she entered. She was, as colleagues and her boss observed, "the whole package." Her business future was bright.

She had two young daughters and a newborn son. She stood at the peak of her career. Soon after her son was born, she shifted her priorities. She decided becoming the next vice president or chief executive officer no longer felt most important to her; instead, she determined to become the best mom she could be.

To almost everyone's astonishment, she resigned her business career to stay at home with her children.

She seemed to have it all.

Her husband, athletic and handsome with a warm laugh and an easy sense of humor, loved his work as an institutional broker. He was a top producer in a small, dynamic firm and was highly respected in the financial industry. He was unusually calm in a volatile business. Clients enjoyed working with him, and many became his close friends. He was very successful. He worked out regularly to stay in shape. He loved his family and treasured their time together. He enjoyed planning special outings and vacations; spending time with his family was a top priority.

He seemed to have it all.

Together, they had it all.

Then things changed. The strong, healthy husband began acting strangely different. Simple things, such as writing a check or spelling simple words, became difficult. He occasionally would lose his balance and stumble. He struggled to understand how to use his cell phone. His upper body began twitching.

The changes were alarming, but as he had done his whole life, he pressed on. The doctors rationalized, "it is just that you are getting older … nothing to be overly concerned about."

Things did not get better. His work, which had been exciting and enjoyable, became frightening and frustrating. Everyone concerned agreed he should go on disability. His interest in sports disappeared. His laughter became less frequent; instead, he displayed an odd seriousness.

He struggled for even the simplest words. He had difficulty dressing himself. He started calling his son by the name of his brother. Sleep became elusive. Then one day, he asked his wife a question, "Where do you live?"

It was as though a knife pierced her heart.

Numerous tests tried to determine what was happening to him. Every medical test result came back normal, except for one brain scan that revealed cloudy white spots. After months of tests, various diagnoses, multiple doctors' visits and trial medications, physicians diagnosed him with a rare brain illness: LewyBody Dementia.

The specialist told the patient's wife that no cause, treatment or cure exists. Life expectancy with this disease is about seven years.

Ultimately, the family's priorities changed drastically. After growing up in a warm, loving and positive environment, the children felt shocked to witness their dad struggle to be "normal."

Suddenly, they realized their roles were changing. Instead of Dad making them laugh, they tried to make Dad laugh. Instead of Dad providing for them, they provided for him. Instead of Dad walking them around the block and protecting them, they protected him as they walked him around the block.

Home never would be the same. Stress and sadness filled the home. Still, the children never wavered in support of their father. Patience, cheerfulness, healthy food and more patience became the order of the day.

She had never pictured herself as her husband's full-time caregiver. No one would choose that path. However, she willingly embraced the role without bitterness or complaint. Every day she walked backwards holding his hands so he could walk forward.

She explained to him and reassured him countless times that she was his wife and that she was not a threat to him. She watched as his once laser-sharp mind struggled to understand even the most basic concept. He could not sleep more than 30 minutes at a time. The family took turns walking him round and round the house, all day and most of the night.

After only three years, he died.

The couple that had it all suddenly had nothing. Their life shifted upside down. The "glue" of their family was gone. Things did not work out as planned.

There would be no Dad at the kids' weddings. The kids would graduate from college without sharing their joy with Dad. Dad would not be coaching his grandkids' baseball teams.

After 32 years of a loving relationship, she was alone at only 54 years old. She felt pain, sorrow and loneliness like never before.

In the meantime …
Five hundred miles away, a guy with a wonderful family, great kids, a loving wife and a comfortable home seemed to have it all. After a stellar career with two Fortune 100 companies, he now was a successful small business owner.

Things seemed to come easily to him. He had been blessed to work for, and with, great people his entire work life. His friends would say he was intense at work, but work challenges never spilled over into his family time. He worked hard at the office and at home.

The father of two daughters and a son, cheering his kids playing soccer, baseball, tennis, basketball and all other activities in which they participated highlighted his weekends. An avid golfer, he also developed close relationships with his golf groups.

On Sundays, he taught a Sunday school class and loved preparing lessons to share with his young adult class.

He seemed to have it all.

His wife was a beautiful, loving and giving person. While the kids were in school, she was a stay-at-home mom. When they became older, she returned to the classroom to give back to her community. She was a great teacher, wife and mom — the "glue" of the family.

Everyone who met her instantly felt her compassion and kindness. She had a ready laugh and an engaging smile for any occasion.

She seemed to have it all.

Together, they had it all.

Then things changed. She was the image of perfect health when she was diagnosed with the rare Inflammatory Breast Cancer — the most aggressive of any of the known breast cancers. The oncologist asked her, "Do you want to live?"

After she confirmed that, indeed, she wanted to live, the doctor then said, "You are in the fight of your life." The prognosis was grim: She had an average life expectancy of five years with a 50 percent chance of living only a year.

Within 12 hours of the diagnosis, she had a port implanted below her collarbone and started chemotherapy. For her husband and her, hearing the words "cancer," "rare" and "aggressive" in the same sentence felt shocking and overwhelming.

His work allowed him to be his wife's caregiver. His schedule instantly became filled with doctors' appointments, hospital stays and trips to the cancer center for chemotherapy.

For two years she fought through chemotherapy, radiation, a mastectomy and more chemotherapy. She beat all odds and was cancer free for seven years. During that time she was blessed to witness the marriages of her children and the births of five grandchildren.

Nine years after her original diagnosis, her cancer returned with a vengeance — this time incurable and inoperable. She lived three more years.

Every night when he put her in bed and until she fell asleep, they talked about the past they cherished and gave thanks for the many experiences they had shared. At the end, just a few weeks before she passed, she miraculously walked down the aisle at her son's wedding, danced the mother/son dance and "partied" with family and friends into the night.

That wedding was the last time most of her friends saw her alive. She said her goodbyes to them; she smiled and told them not to worry, because she would see them again.

Everyone would remember his or her last image of the proud and smiling mother-of-the groom.

When she exhaled her last breath, another couple that had it all suddenly had nothing. Another life shifted upside down. The "glue" of another family was missing.

After 36 years of a loving relationship, he was alone at 58 years old. He felt pain, sorrow and loneliness like never before.

Picking up the pieces

Unknown to the other, at the same time and 500 miles away, the two surviving spouses each tried their best to pick up the pieces of their shattered lives. Even though friends and family wanted to help, there was little anyone could do.

The difficult work of grieving allows no stand-ins. Grief doesn't permit anyone else to shoulder the heaviness for the survivors, particularly for the surviving spouse. More is lost than a spouse. Also lost is the confidant of your most personal conversations, deepest feelings and greatest fears.

The person you celebrated and suffered with is gone. Missing is the one person who knew more about you than anyone else in the world. The loss feels overwhelming.

The phone call

Twenty-five years before, the surviving spouses worked as peers at a Fortune 100 company. During the time they worked together, they each held the other in high regard and felt impressed by the other's character and integrity in their business dealings.

More than 20 years earlier, both had moved on from the company. However, he remained connected to many people in the organization via a message board of ex-employees. One day, he saw a message about her husband's passing.

She did not know of the message board, nor was she aware that one of her friends had posted information about her husband's death.

Grieving and alone, he called her to find out how she was adjusting to the trauma she had experienced. Her husband had passed more than three years before; maybe she could provide advice and encouragement for him in his grief. He found her telephone number on whitepages.com and nervously made the call without knowing what to expect.

She answered the phone. They had not spoken in more than 25 years. Understandably, their first conversation was strange; she did not know he had lost his spouse. They had not kept up with each other and did not realize the parallel paths each of them had traveled.

However, after a few pleasantries, the conversation drifted to their spouses and the lives they had lived together.

Years ago, they casually knew the other's spouse — primarily from company functions. Each of them knew just enough to know her husband and his wife were great people whose lives were taken far too soon. As they spoke, each quickly realized both their spouses had been wonderful partners, parents and friends — both very special people.

Almost instantly, their conversations became meaningful connections between two people who "got it." Each of them had experienced the pain of sickness, hollowness of loss and the sting of death. They understood the suffering, the shattered dreams, the deep family hurt, fear of the future, and the need to talk to someone who could only know these things through a shared experience.

They both "got it."

What had begun as a curiosity call became something to look forward to every night. They liked hearing about people they both knew in the past, but more interesting was talking about the things in their own lives right then.

Both had experienced excruciating emotional pain at the same time; both believed they were the only people in the world facing the challenges of a long illness and the emptiness death brings. Their conversations soon revealed their remarkably similar situations — even the way their children had supported and loved their parents through the toughest of times.

Each soon found themselves eagerly anticipating their 9 o'clock call every evening. What began as a five-minute conversation evolved into several hours each night. Eventually, conversations of the past and their wonderful memories turned to talk about their hopes and the future.

After a couple of months, they set a time to meet in person. He flew to her city, and she met him at the airport. The meeting felt strange for them both. They had seen photographs of each other on social media and had spent hours talking on their nightly calls; now, they stood face to face. The meeting was weird, to say the least.

They left the airport and arrived early for their dinner reservation. They walked along the river and sat on a park bench, where they talked for quite a while. Face-to-face conversation felt different from telephone conversations.

Instead of the easy flow of words, plenty of pauses punctuated their in-person conversation. However they quickly realized that in-person and face-to-face — just like over the phone — the other person "got" it.

That was the beginning.

They did not take long to discover something special together, just like they each had something special apart for many years. Their visits became more frequent. They soon realized being together was much better than connecting over a 500-mile distance by telephone.

Things moved rapidly — some people thought too rapidly. Because of the pain of loss in both families, no criteria existed in which everyone agreed about the "right" time for Mom or Dad to be in a serious relationship.

The couple agreed they wanted to move forward. At the same time, they wanted to be sensitive to their families. Each felt unbelievably grateful to find someone whose conversations were not inhibited by history. In fact, their former marriages enhanced their talks and cemented their relationship.

After just a few months, the two knew clearly they were far better and stronger together than apart. A tsunami-sized shockwave rippled through both families when they announced their engagement and set a wedding date.

Two people felt thrilled and looked forward to their days together. The other members of their families wondered how this coming union would affect their lives. Did they know what they were doing? What about holidays? What about vacations? What about their faith differences? What about our family? Am I going to lose my relationship with my other parent now?

All of these legitimate questions eventually will work themselves out.

The children's dreams of watching their parents grow old together had been shattered. Now, they had to accept the realization that their surviving parent enjoyed spending time with someone other than their mom or dad.

While all of the adult children wanted their parents to move forward, be happy and share their life with another, the reality that their parents could be happy with someone other than their other parent felt foreign and uncomfortable.

Deep down, the kids probably thought this new relationship was disloyal to their mom or dad, now deceased. Their feelings had nothing to do with the new person thrown into their lives; it was just painfully difficult to accept that things would never be like they once had been.

The couple found the situation difficult, as well.

I know. My wife and I are the survivors in that story.

As thrilled as we were about our new beginning, after enjoying 30-plus years of marriage, it felt awkward and strange with someone else. No one could reconcile why things happened as they had.

Plenty of mourning for our late spouses continues, and attacks of grief come without warning. However, we are both convinced that, regardless of the tragedies that lead us to this point, we could and should move forward with a new beginning together.

As we began planning our future together, a few principles became evident to us:

Everything was not lost

It is natural in times of extreme duress to believe everything is lost. My wife and I had to acknowledge that, even in the greatest of tragedies, we did not and have not lost everything.

We had then, and we have now, wonderful families; our spouses had molded our children's character and faith. We wanted to build on their positive influence, not replace them. We could easily see our spouses in each of our children, and we loved what we saw.

The fear of moving forward is a power adversity can create for anyone. Ultimately, my wife and I had to decide to move forward.

Jesus was there to help us take our first step from the tragedy we experienced. "*Come to me, all you who are weary and burdened, and I will give you rest. Take my yoke upon you and learn from me, for I am gentle and humble in heart, and you will find rest for your souls. For my yoke is easy and my burden is light.*"[3]

We took Jesus up on that.

We had to adapt our expectations

Adversity attacks our vision, limits our sights and blinds us with the challenges of the moment. After adversity attacks, we must choose to pull ourselves up, avoid the "why" trap and move forward with positive expectations.

There was no way to answer the "why" questions: Why our spouses? Why the suffering? Why could it not work out differently?

No earthly answers exist for those questions. We just had to get up and move forward. "*No eye has seen, no ear has heard, no mind has conceived what God has prepared for those who love him.*"[4] Our situation was not for us to necessarily understand; we had to experience faith without understanding.

Others could help

To move beyond our adversity, we had to allow God to help us through other people. We both had to independently learn this truth. Sometimes it seemed easier to struggle alone.

We discovered dealing with adversity alone is not the best avenue. Shutting people out contributed to our loneliness. People want to help, but most of the time they have to be invited. Alone, we cannot overcome most challenges we face.

Do not fail to allow others to support you in the ways available to them. You need others to go with you on your journey forward. "*Blessed are those who mourn, for they will be comforted.*"[5] Our friends and family comforted us even without uttering a word. When times are good, your friends know you. During adversity you know your friends.

Permission to move forward

The tragedy that happened to both of our families was unimaginable and incomprehensible. No explanation in this world could reconcile the pain and suffering incurred. However, the survivors could not stop living.

Our children lost one of their parents; they did not deserve to lose the other.

One of the greatest dangers in facing adversity is that we panic, freeze and stop because we perceive the roadblocks, barriers or mountains in our lives as insurmountable. People respond better to crises when they maximize their forward motion. We have to keep moving forward. "*Let us not become weary in doing good, for at the proper time we will reap a harvest if we do not give up.*"[6]

Our spouses would want us to continue doing good things in this world. We had to allow ourselves to move forward.

Celebrate

Celebration feeds our positive energy and our sense of hope. It nourishes our spirits, refreshes our attitudes and gives us strength to fight off the inevitable attacks of negativism and fear that accompany severe adversity. Sometimes, we might have to force ourselves to find something to celebrate.

Regardless of how minor the celebration is, allowing others to celebrate with us is good. "*For I am convinced that neither death nor life, neither angels nor demons, neither the present nor the future, not any powers, neither height nor depth, nor anything else in all creation, will be able to separate us from the love of God that is in Christ Jesus our Lord.*"[7]

We found that even in life's most painful shadows, God will provide a way for us to live our lives to the fullest. We experienced first hand that "*The Lord is close to the brokenhearted and saves those who are crushed in spirit.*"[8]

We never will understand why our tragedies happened to us. No good reason exists to overanalyze why — even though it is tempting. The Bible says, "*For my thoughts are not your thoughts, neither are your ways my ways. As the heavens are higher than the earth, so are my ways higher than your ways and my thoughts than your thoughts.*"[9]

We will never fully understand why — never. We have to trust God and move forward.

We were two very different couples, living 500 miles apart, appearing to have everything, yet we each tragically lost our life's partners. While picking up the pieces, we discovered renewed hope and, indeed, a future.

Granted, we will never see the 50th wedding anniversary we had envisioned with our respective spouses. We always will miss and love our spouses. Those things will not change. However, one of these days, both of our families will gather together and join us in celebrating two 50th anniversaries of being married to two wonderful people.

Our lives have been blessed.

Summary

Every person will face the challenge of overcoming adversity; life's storms will come. Adversity is part of life and has a tendency to blindside you whenever when it shows up. You are never fully prepared.

However, my wife and I discovered we drew closest to God during our deepest suffering. We also acknowledged God was working in powerful ways during our lowest points.

Whether you face personal or professional adversity, you are not the first person to face your problem. Other people have overcome the situation that is consuming your thoughts, energy and hopes.

Remember that from the moment you embark on your journey to overcome adversity, God will guide you and provide you strength if you seek His help. He will be with you through the deep valleys, the raging waters and the consuming fires. He will never, ever leave you or forsake you.

"Trust in the Lord with all your heart and lean not on your own understanding. In all your ways acknowledge him and he will make your paths straight."[10]

God can be trusted.

Questions for Discussion

- ✦ How can you live life to the fullest when you must deal with death, divorce, bankruptcy or any other major adversity?
- ✦ Give an example of Christ's presence during deep suffering.
- ✦ Why is it difficult to accept other people's help during a time of suffering?
- ✦ Is there a time when you can justify being angry while working your way through adversity?
- ✦ What does scripture tell you about heaven? Is it a place you can't wait to get to?
- ✦ When Jesus was lost for three days, see Luke 2:41-52, how do you think Mary and Joseph felt during the time He was missing?

chapter 7

Move Through Exits; Make Grand Entrances

"For our light and momentary troubles are achieving for us an eternal glory that far outweighs them all. So we fix our eyes not on what is seen, but on what is unseen, since what is seen is temporary, but what is unseen is eternal."

– HEBREWS 11:6

Change is good; you go first.

That is a crafty book title, but isn't that the way you feel about most changes in your life? You know the change can be positive and good, but change also requires you to enter the unknown. Why not let someone else go there first?

Most of the time, you don't have that option. The second quarter brings a ton of changes: Family dynamics, job challenges, spiritual questions and movement into the unknown. The second quarter is a supreme faith test.

It is also the time of your life when you can walk through an exit that can lead you running into a grand entrance.

Dream on

Remember Joseph in the Old Testament?[1] He encountered a faith-test supreme while he was living his second quarter. Joseph's father, Jacob, favored and loved him more than any of Joseph's 10 siblings; everyone knew it, too.

Joseph was extra special to Jacob because he was born in Jacob's old age, and he was the first child of his third wife, Rachel. Jacob even gave Joseph an elaborate, beautiful robe symbolic of his love for him. None of the other boys received a robe from their father. You know they had to be thinking and grumbling, "How could this half-brother get all of our father's attention?"

While Joseph's father favored him, his brothers hated him. The brothers would not even say a kind word to him. They believed he was a spy who would tell Daddy everything they were doing. They envied his special treatment. The brothers *hated* him.

Joseph lived the good life. Whatever he wanted, his father provided. He was smart — a dreamer. On one occasion, he had a vivid dream and shared it with his brothers. The dream-share did not go so well.

"Joseph had a dream, and when he told it to his brothers, they hated him all the more. He said to them, 'Listen to this dream I had: We were binding sheaves of grain out in the field when suddenly my sheaf rose and stood upright, while your sheaves gathered around mine and bowed down to it.' His brothers said to him, 'Do you intend to reign over us? Will you actually rule us?' And they hated him all the more because of his dream and what he had said."[2]

Joseph really chapped his brothers. They "hated him all the more."

They probably were thinking, "Yeah, you have quite an imagination if you can dream that we were working together in the field. You don't work; you just prance around in that robe. There is no way we would ever work together."

They hated his dream and hated his interpretation of the dream even more. Who did he think he was?

And Joseph just wouldn't let a sleeping dog lie.

He shared another dream, and it didn't go so well, either: "*Then he had another dream, and he told it to his brothers. 'Listen,' he said, 'I had another dream, and this time the sun and moon and eleven stars were bowing down to me.' When he told his father as well as his brothers, his father rebuked him and said, 'What is this dream you had? Will your mother and I and your brothers actually come and bow down to the ground before you?' His brothers were jealous of him, but his father kept the matter in mind.*"[3]

Obviously, Joseph had not attended charm school. Those who hated him "even more" after the first dream now hated him even more than that!

Things continued on in the family. All the boys, except Daddy's Boy Joseph, were sent to pasture their father's flocks. Joseph stayed home with his father eating, drinking and being merry. After the boys were gone for quite some time, Jacob sent Joseph to check on them and report back to him.

Joseph obeyed and went to find his brothers. He exited the comfort of his home. He entered the unknown. No one could have predicted what was ahead for Joseph.

The brothers saw Joseph headed toward them from afar. They plotted how they would kill him and agreed on the perfect plan.

They would kill Joseph without laying a hand on him. "Let's throw him into an empty pit and let the wild animals do the dirty work. Let's rip that robe to shreds while we are at it."

That is exactly what they did. There Joseph was in the bottom of a pit, humiliated by his brothers. Alone.

What happened to those great dreams?

Joseph's life did not end in the pit. It got even worse. He became a slave, was unfairly accused and entrapped by a king's wife, and he was falsely imprisoned. *You* think life is tough? Joseph knew first-hand how it felt to be humiliated, sold, abandoned, lied about, sexually tempted and locked up.

Yet Joseph never gave up. He never lost his cool. He never lost hope. He kept his faith.

God had not forgotten Joseph. No, God was preparing Joseph for a grand entrance. At age 30, Joseph became the second most powerful leader in all of Egypt. The dreams he had shared with his brothers eventually came true.

He was, indeed, a great leader who exercised authority over his own brothers.

Just as Joseph's dream revealed, his brothers pleaded for Joseph's forgiveness. This was his chance for payback. Remember that pit? Remember when you sold me for 20 pieces of silver? Did you know I spent two years in prison because of you? Payback time.

"But Joseph said to them, 'Don't be afraid. Am I in the place of God? You intended to harm me, but God intended it for good to accomplish what is now being done, the saving of many lives. So then, don't be afraid. I will provide for you and your children.' And he reassured them and spoke kindly to them."[4]

Holy cow! Instead of payback, Joseph spoke kindly to them. Is that the way you would respond? Joseph was mature far beyond his years. Looking backward, he could see that even though he was ridiculed, beaten, hated and set up, God had greater intentions.

Think about this statement, "You intended to harm me, but God intended it for good."

His hurtful exit led to the grand entrance of God's intended good. When you face a hurtful exit, does God have greater intentions for you? Don't bet against it.

Moving through exits

Your exits can lead to grand entrances. When you unexpectedly exit a job, God may have a grand entrance for you in a new environment. When a loved one exits this life, God will help you enter into new hope. When you exit financial security, God will help you enter into a new level of faith and dependence on Him.

During your exits, just as the exit Joseph walked through, God intends them for good to accomplish something greater.

What if the greatest opportunity of your life is just on the other side of the door you face right now marked "EXIT"? Will you believe Jesus can turn whatever you are exiting right now into an entrance of something new and good?

The encouraging news is that beyond every exit can be a grand entrance to the abundance God has set before us.

Exits can be painful. Almost all exits feel stressful. You do not always get to choose the timing or the place. The comfort of familiar surroundings is just that — comfortable. Many people trade love, hugs and safety for hate, beatings and fear because they feel afraid to exit the comfortable. Every exit requires at least a portion of unknown ingredients. However, if you truly believe that every exit could be the beginning of a new grand entrance, you can eliminate a lot of stress as you run toward your entrance.

Exits in the Bible

The Bible helps us understand the exiting process. Most people enjoy stability and comfort. Exits typically represent the opposite — discomfort and instability. Few people enjoy traveling into those regions. Just ask anyone starting a new job, trying to lose weight or giving up smoking.

Exiting can be tough.

Abram was 75 years old when God asked him to exit almost everything he had known in his life.[5] How would you like to be asked to leave your hometown, country, friends and most of your family to go to an unknown land? God asked him to exit his security for insecurity, stability for risk, safety for danger. Those are tough exits.

The call of God involves taking risks and facing insecurities. Following God's will, Abram exited his security and comfort zone and eventually made a grand entrance as the father of the Jewish people.

Involuntary exits

There will be a time when you will face a situation in which you did not create or ask for the exit. It will be unexpected and out of your control. The exit may be unfair, humiliating and frustrating.

Maybe the most dramatic exit of all time happened to Saul.[6] Saul was the man who raised havoc against Jesus. He was the Christian's nightmare — a passionate bully determined to stop Jesus' teachings.

On the road to Damascus to persecute Christians, God touched Saul with a light from heaven, and he fell. For three days, Saul could not see. God sent Ananias to Saul. He placed his hands on Saul, just as the Lord had commanded, and something like scales fell from Saul's eyes.

He could see again! Saul got up and was baptized. He exited his life of persecuting Christians and entered his life as Paul, the man who helped shape the history of Christianity.

Saul did not seek his exit. It totally was involuntary. God provided a grand entrance for him, even though Saul did not know what was happening.

Sometimes, God may force you to exit a place you love and with which you feel comfortable. You may be okay with the status quo; maybe you are even prospering. You don't feel the need to exit, even though it may eventually lead to a grand entrance.

However, circumstances might dictate a change you did not choose. You must enter the unknown. When that happens, you can only increase your trust that God is in control, and your faith that a grand entrance lies straight ahead. Don't allow vengeance, rationalization or blame to become barriers to your grand entrance.

If God leads you to an exit, he will bring you through the entrance. Accept reality — not necessarily the way you wish it to be — and move forward.

Paul addressed this type of change to the church at Philippi, "*But one thing I do: Forgetting what is behind and straining toward what is ahead, I press on toward the goal to win the prize for which God has called me heavenward in Christ Jesus.*"[7]

The use of the word "straining" is interesting. Would he have to strain if it were easy? Would he have to strain if he felt content with current circumstances?

When change happens, strain toward what is ahead and press on.

Lessons from a mouse

Several years ago, scientists evaluated mice and their reaction to change. They laid four tubes side-by-side on the floor. They placed a cube of cheese in the second tube. The scientists released the mouse, and it immediately went to the first tube. Finding the tube empty, the mouse proceeded to the second tube. There he discovered and ate the cube of cheese, which met his basic need for survival. The mouse then returned to his point of release.

The next day, the mouse followed the same routine by going to the empty first tube, eating cheese from the second tube, and returning to his point of release. He repeated the same routine for several days.

Finally, realizing that he was wasting time by going to the first tube, the mouse traveled directly to the second tube. He ate the cheese, met his need for survival and went back. This routine also continued for several days.

Then, the people conducting the experiment moved the cheese to the third tube. The next day, the mouse went directly to the second tube where his needs always had been met — but no cheese.

How do you think the mouse responded? Did he go back to the first tube looking for the cheese? No. Did he go back to where he started? No. Did he go to the third tube searching for the cheese? No.

He chose to stay in the second tube — where his needs had always been met — and waited for the cheese to come back to him. If allowed, the mouse would have starved in the tube as he waited for the cheese; instead, he should have responded to the change.

Doesn't this sound like the reaction of some people you know? "Let's wait," they say. "We have always done it this way. It worked in the past."

We can learn two points from this story:

First, if your situation changes — even though your needs always have been met and you feel comfortable with the old way — respond to the change. Don't be stuck in the same place and blame others for the change. You cannot improve without change.

Technology has made us acutely aware that change makes us uncomfortable, but it also has demonstrated that change eventually leads to improvement. You have to move forward and run toward a new entrance. The changes in technology have made our lives better in most cases. Remember roaming charges? Cell phones that only made/received calls (dumb phones)? Rabbit ears? Home phones with cords? Typewriters? Who wants to walk back through any of those exits?

Exits are not unique to technology, though. Look around. Look at your workplace … or your family and friends. Many exits have taken place, which have led to grand entrances.

Even family traditions exit. Family traditions are important, but as my family has grown, we have had to make adjustments to our traditions. With our kids' and grandkids' schedules, we can't be together every holiday. We have exited that phase of our life and entered into the "enjoying fully the time that we have together" phase. I can't worry about the exit from our old traditions; I have to adapt to and embrace the entrance to our new and different traditions.

If you are waiting for things to be like they used to be, you could wind up starving like the mouse, or you may feel just plain miserable. Your past is important, but don't allow it to eat your future. Ponder your past long enough to learn from your mistakes, and then move forward.

When your exit happens, don't sit and wait — look for your grand entrance.

The second lesson to be learned from the experiment is that while your needs are being met, keep looking for ways to improve. A whole block of cheese could have been in the fourth tube, and the mouse would not have known because he felt content with his little cube.

Make improvements while things are going well. Your attitude is better, stress is less, and your thought process is sharper.

The bottom line: When things are going well, keep looking for more cheese.

Exits are here to stay

Exits will not go away. In fact, you probably will have to adjust to more exits in the next 10 years than you already have seen in your lifetime. Those are new entrances for you. Be prepared. Your reaction to exits and your attitude during your entrance will have a major impact on your success and happiness.

When you have control over your exit, check yourself. Is exiting the right thing to do for the right reason? Have you diligently prayed about the exit? Has the Holy Spirit confirmed to you that you need to exit where you are and enter into a new beginning? Have your trusted advisors confirmed that you are exiting for the right reasons?

If so, get going. Exits lead to grand entrances when you follow God's plan for you.

Summary

Did you ever walk into a movie early and see the last 10 minutes of the show? You watch the end of the movie as the hero and heroine head into their life of happiness. All you see is the outcome.

When you re-watch the movie from the beginning, your perception is completely different, because you know what happens in the end. Your stress level is down, you can relax, and you can enjoy the scary scenes; you already know everything will be okay.

We already know the end of the story, too. Christ has won the battle for us. As you work your way through exits, keep focused on your ultimate grand entrance ahead.

Spend your energy focusing on the next entrance rather than fixating on the last exit. "*Let us not become weary of doing good, for at the proper time we will reap a harvest if we do not give up.*"[8]

Miracles. That's what Jesus does. He turns our painful exits into grand entrances.

Questions for discussion

- How did Joseph keep his faith when he was humiliated, sold, abandoned, lied about and locked up? What would you do?
- How do you think his brothers reacted when they recognized Joseph years later?
- How did Saul react to his involuntary exit? Did he fixate on his past?

- ✦ What are some examples of big exits and entrances in your life?

- ✦ Everyone has unexpected exits. How can you make the best of your next unexpected exit?

- ✦ What does it mean to look for more cheese when you have enough to survive? How does the cheese story relate to Jesus' parable about talents? (Matthew 25:14-30)

chapter 8

Stand Firm

"Therefore, my dear brothers and sisters, stand firm. Let nothing move you. Always give yourselves fully to the work of the Lord, because you know that your labor in the Lord is not in vain."
– 1 Corinthians 15:58

The second quarter is a period of movement. People move from jobs, towns, churches and friends. It can be a scary time. Your kid's college tuition payments are just around the corner. Teenagers test your patience, faith and everything else in your being. Job opportunities intrigue you. Your marriage exited the honeymoon phase. Carrots dangle in front of you that previously had not caught your eye.

The second quarter is a time to stand firm on your values.

The offer of a lifetime

During the 1980s and 1990s, Georgia Tech was a college baseball powerhouse. Following the leadership of Coach Jim Morris, the Yellow Jackets were the only NCAA team to reel off nine straight years of participating in the NCAA Championship tournament. During that nine-year stretch, the team won more than 400 games … clearly among the elite programs in the NCAA.

Rick Jones served as the top assistant at Georgia Tech from 1990 until the end of the 1993 season. During those four seasons, Georgia Tech won 180 games. After being the head coach at two small colleges before he joined the Jackets, Jones served as the right-hand man for Jim Morris. A 40-year-old fireball, Rick Jones was the logical choice to become the Georgia Tech head coach if Coach Morris decided to retire or leave Tech for any reason.

In August of 1993, Tulane University offered its head baseball position to Rick Jones. Tulane was not exactly a powerhouse at that time — having won only seven NCAA tournament games since 1937. Jones evaluated the situation. Jim Morris had no plans to retire, and there was no guarantee he would be offered the Georgia Tech head job even if he did.

Rick Jones accepted the head baseball coach position for the Tulane Green Wave team.

In September, one month after Jones accepted the Tulane job, the Miami Hurricane head coach job unexpectedly opened. Miami was the only school in the entire country that would entice Jim Morris to leave Georgia Tech.

Coach Morris was offered and accepted his dream job — head coach at The University of Miami.

Rick Jones remained the obvious choice to replace Morris, even though he now was at Tulane. Everyone thought he would come back home and coach the Yellow Jackets. After all, he had not yet permanently moved his family to New Orleans.

Even the Tulane players thought he would go back to Tech. Who could blame him? His dream job — a top-10 college coaching job — and his comfortable surroundings probably awaited him if he wanted to go back home and coach Georgia Tech.

Before Jones could officially interview for any job, he needed permission from Tulane's athletic director, Kevin White. Jones arranged a meeting with White. As soon as he walked into White's office, White began the conversation, "I thought you might be coming to see me. I worked so hard to get you here."

Before he could say anything else, Jones interrupted, "I am not going anywhere. I want to stop the rumors of my departure right now. I am your baseball coach at Tulane."

A Tulane team meeting was called, and everyone expected Jones to say thanks but no thanks to the team. Instead, he walked in and quickly announced that Tulane was his team, and it was time to get to work.

The decision shocked his team. Its attitude immediately changed. If Tulane was worth Coach Jones' turning down the Georgia Tech opportunity, maybe the team was better than it thought. Maybe Rick Jones saw something in the players they could not see.

The following season, Tulane won 41 games and made the NCAA tournament. Jones went on to coach at Tulane for 21 seasons, won 818 games and played in the NCAA tournament 12 times; Tulane made the College World Series twice.

Rick Jones compiled the best record of any coach in Tulane baseball history and represented the University with class and dignity; the NCAA did not even once sanction him.

Rick Jones had the courage to stand firm. He left his familiar, successful surroundings and followed his instincts. He stood up to the commitment he made to his team and the university. He resisted the temptation of taking the easiest route and staying at Georgia Tech.

He had the courage to stand firm and do what was right, even when it was hard.

Courage vs. Fear

The word "courage" comes from the French word "coeur," which means heart. Courage is the attitude of facing and dealing with anything recognized as dangerous, difficult or painful instead of withdrawing from it.

The relationship between courage and fear is interesting. For some, courage means not feeling fear at all. "Courage," said Mark Twain, is "resistance to fear, mastery of fear — not absence of fear."

We walk forward along a path; fear is there, too. We keep walking.

Standing firm means having the guts, nerve and heart to do things differently and allowing progress to develop. Improvement does not happen by taking the path of least resistance and conforming to the way things have always been.

The opposite of courage is conformity — keep doing the same ol' same ol' … and keep getting the same ol' same ol.'

Courageous leaders standing firm

In Gideon's battle with the Midianites,[1] Gideon probably felt pretty good about going into the battle with 32,000 soldiers. They were prepared, ready and confident. With 32,000 soldiers, they could overpower the opponent and give themselves credit for a victory.

God had other plans. "*Gideon, you have too many men — Israel may think they won with their own strength. Let the ones that want to leave, go.*"

Twenty-two thousand had no desire to stick around. Ten thousand remained. God said, "*There are still too many, take them to the water and I will sift them out for you.*"

This time only 300 men remained to fight the battle.

Imagine how Gideon felt. When he had 32,000 soldiers, courage came easily; anyone could lead 32,000 to victory. Now he had to go into battle with only 300. Stand firm? All of a sudden, the game had changed. The challenge became more than a battle; it was a test of courage and faith.

Gideon had to stand firm on his faith in God. God allowed Gideon to slip into the enemy camp and overhear a conversation that confirmed God would deliver the camp to Gideon and his men. God provided the plan, and Gideon stood firm and carried it out against all odds.

As a youth, David stood firm for what he knew was right. He did not view Goliath as a giant, but rather as someone who mocked God — an unacceptable stance. David stood firm and trusted God. "*The Lord who delivered me from the paw of the lion, and the paw of the bear will deliver me from the hand of this Philistine.*"[2] When all of his associates were afraid to take a stand for God, David displayed total trust in God. He had the courage to do what was right, even though his peers discouraged him from trusting God completely.

Barnabas stood firm to support Saul and let the disciples know Saul had changed and had become a disciple of Jesus. Barnabas took Saul to the disciples and stood up for him when everyone else was afraid.[3] Without Barnabas' courage, Paul's ministry would have been much more difficult to begin.

Paul stood firm to preach for Jesus. After his life radically changed, Paul shared the gospel soon after he had persecuted others for preaching the gospel. After Paul's conversion, people looked at him skeptically, and there even was a conspiracy to kill him. Paul still had the courage to stand firm and accept his new role; he led thousands to Jesus.[4]

Stand firm and persevere

Times existed when Jesus felt weary and struggled to complete His mission.[5] His heart hurt so much that He cried. He felt frustrated, mad, betrayed, and He needed rest and time to pray.

When you feel like giving up on your mission, remember He felt that way, too … and He is with you now.

When I began my business, success did not come easily or quickly. In fact, at one point, I thought about giving up. Then, God provided a way for me to sustain, grow and prosper.

As I pondered my next career move, I received a call from a business acquaintance, Mark Layton. I had known Mark during my time at FedEx, where he was a client. But we were not particularly close; in fact, I had not seen him in years.

His call came at a time when my business struggled. Mark asked me to speak at a conference his company was sponsoring in Washington D.C. I agreed; I thought this might be the last meeting where I would represent CornerStone.

Little did I know what God had planned for me.

After my speech at the conference, Mark suggested we meet to discuss his business. During the next couple of weeks, Mark and I met several times that ultimately resulted in him hiring me to train his company's managers worldwide. The training would last at least six months. His phone call, our meetings and the training contract allowed me to sustain my business long enough to gather enough traction to move forward.

If I had created a list of 100 people I thought would be the person to have that kind of impact on my life and business, Mark Layton might not have made the list. However, he was No. 1 on God's list for me at that time and place in my life.

The story did not end there. As Paul Harvey would say, "and, now, the rest of the story."

Several weeks after I began working with Mark's team, I received a call from Kim from Phoenix. I had no idea who she was when I returned her call. Almost immediately into the conversation, she said she believed I was the answer to her prayers.

Surprised by her comment, I asked why. She told me she was Mark Layton's sister and that she had been praying for years that a Christian man would come along and provide a positive influence for Mark. She was convinced I was that man.

Who could have put that plan together? Certainly not me. God provided Mark for my business growth and me for Mark's spiritual growth — all at the same time without either of us realizing it.

Don't be surprised whom God uses at the right time and place if you have the courage to stand firm and follow God's will for you.

Stand firm and stand up

When you have struggled in a situation for a while, it may be easy to become complacent and lie around feeling sorry for yourself. Many people give up and quit right before their blessing. Your courage ultimately is measured by how much it takes to discourage you enough to quit.

Stand firm.

In the Bible, there is a story of a man who had been sick for 38 years.[6] His situation must have appeared hopeless to him. Every day he would lie on his mat by the porch of the pool of Bethesda. Other blind, lame or paralyzed people surrounded him; everyone hoped for a miracle.

One day, Jesus saw him and knew he had been ill a long time. He asked him a simple question: "Would you like to get well?"

That may be the easiest question to answer ever. "Of course" would be the obvious answer. But the man did not answer Jesus that way. Instead of "YES," he began his list of excuses: "*I can't sir. I have no one to put me into the pool. Someone always gets there ahead of me.*"

The question was so simple: Would you like to get well?

He never answered it.

Jesus' response was not to commiserate with the man and agree how bad the situation had been for 38 long, suffering years. He simply said, "*Stand up, pick up your mat, and walk. Instantly the man was healed. He rolled up his mat and began walking.*"

It takes courage to stand up, roll up your mat and get moving. Blaming others for your situation does not take courage. In fact, placing blame is cowardly.

Would you like to get well? That could be the simple question God asks you. He will give you the path to follow.

Stand firm or let go

Many people face this decision somewhere in their career: "Do I continue, or is it best to let go of the dream?"

Perseverance could lead to bankruptcy, or perseverance could lead to God using a person from out of the blue in your life — just as

He did in mine.

How do you know whether to persevere or let go? No one can answer that question for you. God will only make your answer clear through consistent prayer for direction.

You need to answer three questions:

1. How is God directing your life? Are you getting closer to or further away from the person you want to be?
2. Are all signs to keep going, or is it just a dream not based on God's will for your life?
3. What do your trusted advisors and counselors say?

In my experience, friends and family members do not make great counselors. They want you to succeed and follow your dream. They don't want to hurt your feelings. And, most of the time, they do not have enough experience in the area to provide good advice anyway.

I have found that my best advisors have been casual acquaintances. They are people who have more experience than I do and they will tell me the truth from their perspectives, even if it hurts my feelings.

My business mentor was the late Fred Smith, Sr., a businessman and author who lived in Dallas. We did not know each other until a friend recommended I call him. We hit it off well, but to say that Mr. Smith was brutally honest is an understatement. I forever will be grateful for the wisdom he provided me during a two-year period to discern the path I needed to follow.

If you have diligently prayed the matter through, sought wise counsel and the answer is to stay the course, cling to the promise: *"Do not be afraid; do not be discouraged. Go out to face them tomorrow, and the Lord will be with you."*[7]

If the answer from your prayers and wise counsel is to let go of the dream, have the courage to let it go and accept God's will for you.

Stand firm with others

Standing firm alone is difficult. You know what you should do, but under duress, you need others to stand with you.

If you've been to a dry, arid climate like Arizona or West Texas, you've probably seen tumbleweeds all over the place; they blow here and there in all different directions.

Tumbleweed is an above ground plant that, once mature and dry, disengages from the root and tumbles away in the wind. When the wind blows from the west, the tumbleweed will go east. When the wind blows from the east, it goes west. It does not control where it goes — the wind is in charge.

In contrast to the tumbleweed stands a redwood tree. Have you ever seen a magnificent redwood tree? Growing over 300 feet tall — higher than the length of a football field — redwood trees tower above all other trees. Most of them have scars on their trunks that reflect tough times; some even have huge caverns carved through their trunks by wildfire.

But still they grow. Redwoods are full of life; it's difficult to kill one.

The secret to the redwood's amazing ability to survive and endure is not in the tree itself. Redwoods grow in clusters. Their strength is their root system, but not a typical independent root system that grows downward.

You might think that redwoods grow so tall because of their deep roots; but, in fact, they have no taproot, and their roots might reach no deeper than six to 12 feet. For every foot in height, the redwood tree sends its roots three times that distance — not down, but out. If the tree is 300 feet tall, its roots reach out 900 feet, intertwining with roots from the other redwoods in the grove.

Redwoods can withstand the elements and even the ravages of fire because they connect with other redwoods in the grove. The roots in a redwood grove interweave so tightly that it's impossible to tell which roots belong to which tree.

Standing alone, an individual redwood easily would fall; but intertwined and standing together, they strengthen and support one another. Each tree is independent, but they all connect through their roots by a common goal — survival.

Your faith walk is similar. If you stand alone, not connected with other Christians, your faith probably resembles the tumbleweed — subject to the current circumstances you face. You put your trust in humans rather than stand firm and put your trust in God. Connecting with others will help hold up your faith.

Stand firm and trust

It takes courage to stand firm and look beyond the current situation into hope and to trust that God will provide for us. In Chuck Swindoll's terrific book, "*Hope Again*,"[8] he states, "Hope is a wonderful gift from God, a source of strength and courage in the face of life's harshest trials." God's gift of hope looks like this:

- ✦ When we are trapped in a tunnel of misery, hope points to the light at the end.
- ✦ When we are overworked and exhausted, hope gives us fresh energy.
- ✦ When we feel discouraged, hope lifts our spirits.
- ✦ When we feel tempted to quit, hope keeps us going.
- ✦ When we lose our way and confusion blurs the destination, hope dulls the edge of panic.

- ✦ When we struggle with a crippling disease or a lingering illness, hope helps us persevere beyond the pain.
- ✦ When we fear the worst, hope reminds us God is still in control.
- ✦ When we must endure the consequences of bad decisions, hope fuels our recovery.
- ✦ When we find ourselves unemployed, hope tells us we still have a future.
- ✦ When we are forced to sit back and wait, hope gives us the patience to trust.
- ✦ When we feel rejected and abandoned, hope reminds us we are not alone — we'll make it.
- ✦ When we say our final farewell to someone we love, hope in the life beyond carries us through grief.

The Bible promises: "*Those who hope in the Lord will renew their strength. They will soar on wings like eagles. They will run and not grow weary; they will walk and not be faint.*"[9]

Stand firm and trust God's wonderful gift of hope.

Summary

Ultimately, the true measurement of success is being able to look in the mirror and know you had the courage to stand firm and do what you believed God willed for your life. The Bible teaches the ultimate reward for having such courage: "*So do not throw away your confidence; it will be richly rewarded. You need to persevere so that when you have done the will of God, you will receive what he has promised.*"[10]

More than 20 times, Jesus commanded, "Fear not." It takes courage to stand firm and trust Jesus when we are afraid, unsure and lack confidence in ourselves. The best God has for us often is not far beyond what we fear the most.

"Therefore put on the full armor of God, so that when the day of evil comes, you may be able to stand your ground, and after you have done everything, to stand. Stand firm then, with the belt of truth buckled around your waist, with the breastplate of righteousness in place, and with your feet fitted with the readiness that comes from the gospel of peace. In addition to all this, take up the shield of faith, with which you can extinguish all the flaming arrows of the evil one. Take the helmet of salvation and the sword of the Spirit, which is the word of God."[11]

Stand firm.

Questions for Discussion

- ✦ Rick Jones took a firm stand that worked out well for him. Why do you think he stayed at Tulane instead of going back to Georgia Tech?
- ✦ How do you know when it is time to persevere or time to let go?
- ✦ How can you develop "redwood" friends?
- ✦ Why is there a broad and accepted culture of silence, instead of standing firm?
- ✦ Does political correctness have an effect on your ability to stand firm?

chapter 9

Give Peace a Chance

"If it is possible, as far as it depends on you, live at peace with everyone."
– Romans 12:16

Peace in the second quarter.

That sounds good, but the second quarter probably will be the least peaceful time of your life. You can try your best to live in peace, but maybe those around you battle against peace.

During the second quarter, life's stress makes it difficult to cultivate peace with God. Family and friend issues tend to magnify themselves, so peace with others becomes difficult, too. You might have trouble gaining peace with yourself because of your own insecurities.

The agony of living in turmoil will hang on until you face the issues keeping peace away.

Finding peace and living in peace during your second quarter will make life more pleasant at halftime and for the rest of your life.

Nightmare

Do you ever have a recurring dream? Maybe you dream about something that happened a long time ago that continues to haunt you. Maybe your dream is something that never happened but strangely still appears as an occasional nightmare.

I have a recurring dream about my college days. At least once a year, I dream that during my senior year, I go to take the final exam in my Real Estate Finance class. When I reach the classroom, no one is there. The class had moved to another building early in the semester; I did not know, because I had not attended class since the first day.

In my dream, I could not graduate.

I wake up in a cold sweat and realize it was only a dream. I graduated from college decades ago. There are some nuggets of truth in that dream — maybe I should have attended that class more often. I guess that's why the dream hangs on for decades.

Many people live real-life recurring nightmares. Some involve their relationship with God. Some involve stressed relationships with other people. Others' recurring nightmares reflect the lack of grace and peace with themselves.

Is anything in your life stealing your peace?

If you do not have peace with God, peace with others and peace with yourself, you cannot live life to the fullest. Something will always create internal chaos and prevent you from becoming the person you want to be.

Peace with God

How can you have peace with God? Your peace with God largely will dictate the way you handle the second-quarter experiences of your life. Every chapter in this book deals with that basic question, especially chapter 5 – Pray Like There is No Tomorrow.

Paul's final instruction to the Phillippians was on how to receive God's peace: "*Whatever is true, whatever is noble, whatever is right, whatever is pure, whatever is lovely, whatever is admirable — if anything is excellent or praiseworthy — think about such things. Whatever you have learned or received or heard from me, or seen in me — put into practice. And the God of peace will be with you.*"[1]

That's the formula: Dwell on God's blessings. Apply Biblical lessons. Receive God's peace.

Prolific Christian author C.S. Lewis wrote, "To walk out of the will of God is to step into nowhere." When you venture from God's path for your life, you leave peace. It is impossible to have peace with God outside of His will.

If you know who you want to be, but you are becoming someone else, you will not feel at peace. He is waiting and will give you peace when you seek it. "*Humble yourselves therefore, under God's mighty hand, that he may lift you up in due time. Cast all your anxiety on him because he cares for you.*"[2]

Seek peace with God.

Peace with others

In an unpeaceful situation with someone, you must have a complete understanding of what led to the discord. I am sure you have seen two people in furious disagreement about what they think the other is thinking.

How do they know what the other is thinking? They are disagreeing without taking the time to truly understand the issue. You can never make peace with others that way.

A problem accurately stated is almost solved; the challenge is figuring out the real problem. The Bible says: "*Get the facts at any price, and hold on tightly to all the good sense you can get,*"[3] and "*He who answers without listening, that is his folly and shame.*"[4]

Sometimes you must use all your energy to tightly hold onto good sense while gathering the facts. Listen, question and discover the real issue. "*The first to present his case seems right, till another comes forward and questions him.*"[5] You can resolve most issues pretty easily when you and the other person agree on the true problem.

Don't waste time making peace with the wrong issue.

Molehills to Mountains

What happens if you ignore a conflict with other people? Does the conflict magically fix itself or disappear? Of course it doesn't. Instead, the conflict takes on a new life, and grows bigger and bigger.

Major conflicts typically begin as a minor issue, but both parties allow the problem to simmer into something totally out of control.

If you look back, the mountain-size conflicts in your life most likely began as molehills you failed to address. Ignoring a molehill does not make it go away; it continues to get larger and larger. Ignore it long enough, and eventually the molehill becomes a mountain that will block the path of peace with the other person.

Maybe you have heard the concept called the 1-10-100 rule — or the "molehills to mountains rule." Loosely translated, the longer a conflict exists without being addressed, the more harmful, expensive and time-consuming it is to fix.

For example, if two people solve a conflict quickly and efficiently, the equivalent of one unit of time, money or resources is necessary to solve it. Peace comes quickly.

If two people ignore that same problem, it will grow; then they require the equivalent of 10 units to solve the problem. Peace is harder to find. The larger problem creates more emotions and perceptions to address.

And if the two people allow the conflict to continue, the wounds become deeper and tougher to fix. The conflict will take at least 100 units to solve. That is 100 times what it would have cost to solve the same conflict in the beginning.

One hundred times harder to find peace.

The molehills-to-mountains rule can apply in many situations: An adversarial conflict between family members, a misperception between friends, an issue between spouses addressed only by silence, or a simple lack of communication.

Each issue has two things in common: They negatively impact every person they touch, and rather than fix themselves, they "snowball" over time. You probably have seen minor situations become major catastrophes because the parties involved ignored the problem; they hoped it would mysteriously disappear.

Problems never mysteriously disappear.

When the conflict is personal and emotional

One exception exists to "solving the conflict immediately," or the molehills to mountains rule: Personal, emotional involvement.

In this case, wisely put time between the situation and your response. Avoid defending yourself or addressing the problem immediately when you have been personally attacked.

Every person, regardless of age or success, will face having to respond to adversity between himself and someone about whom he cares deeply. No one is immune. However, few will face a situation as challenging as this one in the Bible:

While David and his warriors were away to fight a battle, the enemy attacked and burned their village. The enemy also took captive the soldiers' wives, sons and daughters. Imagine a scene so horrible that these strong warriors "*wept aloud until they had no strength left to weep.*"[6]

The men blamed David for their tragic loss; after all, he was their leader. They conspired to stone him. You can almost feel David's pain. His own family also had been captured, and now his soldiers had turned on him.

Yet, even in this tragic situation, David kept his cool and put some time and space between the conflict and his response. He left to seek a quiet place to sort through the issues, and he "*found strength in the Lord his God.*"[7]

During his time of prayer and solitude, he found a new course of action that led to a solution. Much wisdom lies in the practice of "sleeping on a problem," especially when the conflict is personal. Follow David's example the next time you face such a conflict.

Keep your cool, don't panic, go to a quiet place, and seek God's direction for solutions to your problem. Then follow the Bible's guidance: "*Everyone should be quick to listen, slow to speak and slow to become angry. For man's anger does not bring about the righteous life that God desires.*"[8]

Again, keep your cool, don't panic, go to a quiet place and seek God's direction.

Ask for forgiveness

You will not find peace without seeking forgiveness. Whether you need to forgive yourself, forgive others or ask someone for forgiveness, pursue forgiveness for your own peace. If anyone perceives you hurt him or her, ask for forgiveness.

A simple question — will you forgive me? — releases you from the chains of unspoken, unforgiving hurt.

The Bible says: "*Blessed are the peacemakers, for they will be called sons of God.*"[9] Also James provides this encouragement: "*And those who are peacemakers will plant seeds of peace and reap a harvest of righteousness.*"[10] Those verses mentioned nothing about peace *lovers*. Everyone loves peace. Few thrive on creating conflicts. But the blessed people do more than love peace.

Blessed people are peace*makers*.

Yes, but…

What about forgiving someone who wounded you? This person damaged your relationship or reputation, or he attacked your personal beliefs. He should ask *you* for forgiveness, not the other way around. He is obviously the problem, right? Maybe he is, but maybe he isn't.

Before you ask forgiveness, pray about the issue to discern whether you might have contributed to the problem. If so, go to the person, admit your part in the problem, and then ask forgiveness.

Even though he wounded you, "Blessed is the peacemaker."

You are the peacemaker.

Jesus set a pretty high bar for peacemakers. When Peter asked, "*Lord, how many times shall I forgive my brother when he sins against me? Up to seven times? Jesus said to him, 'Not seven times, but, I tell you, seventy-seven times.'"*[11]

In other words, forgive as many times as it takes. Humble yourself and make peace through forgiveness; forgiveness is the very core of a humble heart. Accept that you may never know all the facts of the current situation. Leave the judging to Jesus.

Is a current relationship missing something because of unforgiveness? The cost of living with a fractured relationship is an enormously heavy burden to carry around. Wherever you go, you carry it with you. It saps your energy, consumes your thoughts and paralyzes you from moving forward. It is like a dark cloud hovering over you; it follows you and will not go away. Forgiveness is the first step to healing.

While dying on the cross, Jesus forgave the very people who hung him there. "*Father, forgive them; for they know not what they are doing.*"[12] They beat him beyond recognition, crowned him with thorns and nailed him to the cross. Yet, in the midst of it all, Jesus forgave.

Maybe you need to wrestle up the nerve to humbly ask someone to forgive you.

Forgiveness is one of the best gifts you can give yourself and the other person. Give your gift away. Forgiveness is not a loan with collateral or a payback schedule attached to it. It is not a trade. "*Forgive them as quick as you can and try to let go of your anger. Get rid of all bitterness, rage and anger, brawling and slander, along with every form of malice. Be kind and compassionate to one another, forgiving each other, just as in Christ God forgave you.*"[13]

Forgiveness is a gift given without attachments.

You may prefer to pay back the person who hurt you by hurting him. That is a natural response. However, the Bible says to do just the opposite. It says to "*repay evil with blessing.*"[14]

What would it hurt if you called right now and asked for forgiveness? You may not believe that is your responsibility, but do it for yourself. Forgiveness is a gift you give yourself.

If that person chooses not to accept your gift, you did your part.

Blessed is the peacemaker. That can be you.

Peace with yourself

If you are breathing, you probably are your toughest critic. Of course, you know yourself best, and you naturally tend to focus on your weaknesses rather than your strengths.

Why do you do that? You are God's child. Why should you be so hard on yourself?

Because you are human.

Thoughts and actions outside of who you want to be are not unique to you. You are human. Every saint has a past, and every sinner has a future. No sin is unique to you. "*For all have sinned and come short of the glory of God.*"[15]

God will forgive you. If you have confessed, God has forgiven you. Why can't you forgive yourself?

I enjoy reading Christmas letters from friends each year. I am interested to know what is going on in their lives. Most of the time, the letters only contain the positive things that happened. People generally do not want to share the challenges that came first.

That is okay; most of us want to hear the good stuff. However, if you look back at your friends' letters through the years, all look similar. One year, the letter brags about Jane and John living the good life. The next year's letter talks about Jane's new boyfriend. One year Joe is going to college; the next year he is living at home — what a blessing!

You know what I mean. No one is perfect, even if the Christmas letter or Facebook post attempts to fool you otherwise.

Don't measure yourself against what you *think* others may have. It is probably not as good as you think. Measure yourself by the ways in which you seek to become the person you want to be. That is completely under your control. Actively pursuing your personal mission will bring you peace.

Let go of any unforgiven load you carry. Become a peacemaker. Love yourself as God loves you.

Summary

We all will have some good and some not-so-good things happen this year. Same as last year, the year before and next year, as well. People who live life to the fullest have learned to enjoy peace even in tough times.

Peace with God. Peace with others. Peace with themselves. The peace that transcends all understanding is available to you, as well. "***And the peace of God, which transcends all understanding,*** *will guard your hearts and your minds in Christ Jesus.*"[16]

Questions for Discussion

- ✦ "When you venture from God's path for your life, you leave peace." What are some examples of leaving God's path?
- ✦ Can you give an example of when you experienced the molehills to mountains rule in your life?
- ✦ Read 1 Samuel 30:1-6. How would you feel if you were David?
- ✦ Do you have friendships that prevent peace? What can you do about it?
- ✦ Are you carrying a grudge that is bigger than the one that Jesus could have carried while hanging on the cross? How did He respond? How do you respond?
- ✦ Why are you so hard on yourself?

chapter 10

Be All In, All the Time

"We instructed you how to live in order to please God, as in fact you are living. Now, we ask you and urge you in the Lord Jesus to do this more and more."
– 1 THESSALONIANS 4:1

More and more.

The second quarter is the time to think about and establish your life goals. You may have lived a life that is pleasing to God, but now is the time to do more and more ... not less and less.

The good news is that the more you continue to give to others, the more you receive from others. Get committed now to the important things in life, set your goals, and serve others as you become the person you want to be.

Resolutions

Most people enjoy turning the calendar to begin a new year. It's a chance to start fresh with a renewed purpose. Many people make New Year's resolutions to ensure the best year ever: Lose weight, read more, maintain a better attitude; you name it, and people are resolving to do it. Hope rises and warms everyone's heart. Surely perfection is finally within reach.

Perhaps most common, people resolve to exercise more and get in shape. Off to the gym you go. Workout facilities can be so crowded in January, you might have to wait for a machine to work out; everybody wants to get in shape.

However, by April, a dogsled team could train with you on the empty treadmills. The people in January were mostly *interested* people. A few months later, only the *all-in* people remain.

Why do your grand ambitions fade to invisibility? Usually, life gets in the way, but you knew that when you started. You have the desire. You genuinely want to improve, but maybe you discovered you were not prepared to pay the price.

A yawning chasm lives between interest and all in. You don't have to pay a price to be interested. But all in demands you move beyond interested and commit yourself.

Beyond halfway

No one wants to be around people who are some in, some of the time. Who wants to have friends who fluctuate based on their moods or whatever happened to them last night?

People feel comfortable when they undoubtedly know the commitments of others, even if they do not agree with them. The wishy-washy, lukewarm people are the ones who drive everybody crazy.

Jesus addressed the middle-of-the road people: "*I know your deeds, that you are neither cold nor hot. I wish you were either one or the other! So because you are lukewarm — neither hot nor cold — I am about to spit you out of my mouth."*[1] Everyone understands Jesus' analogy. Few enjoy the disgusting taste of lukewarm water. An all-in Christian cannot follow Jesus halfway.

You can't be the person you want to be without being all in, all the time. No middle ground exists. To go all in, all the time with Christ is personal. Are you ready to be all in, all the time — no matter what?

All in on the gurney

In 1921, Dr. Evan O'Neill Kane made history at Kane Summit Hospital in Pennsylvania. A veteran surgeon, Kane performed an appendectomy using local anesthesia for the first time. Dr. Kane was a crusader for local anesthesia; he contended it was far safer than the conventional method of general anesthesia. Not many of his colleagues believed his theory and felt reluctant to test it on their patients. They needed proof.

Dr. Kane's patients did not express excitement to be part of a laboratory study, either. After several weeks of searching for a volunteer to prove his theory, the surgeon finally found a candidate who was willing to test the theory while undergoing an appendectomy.

At the time of the surgery, staff prepped and wheeled the patient into the surgical suite. Dr. Kane then took the scalpel and performed the surgery. The procedure went as planned, and the patient complained only of minor discomfort.

Two days after the procedure, the hospital dismissed the patient. Thanks to the brave volunteer, Dr. Kane demonstrated that local anesthesia was not only a viable alternative to general anesthesia, but even better.

Who courageously volunteered for Dr. Kane's experimental surgery?

Dr. Kane! He performed the first surgery using local anesthesia on himself.

He was so committed to his belief that he was willing to become a patient just to convince other patients to trust their doctor. Everyone else was interested in knowing whether the procedure would work … Dr. Kane was all in to find out himself.

Are you passionate enough about your personal, professional and spiritual beliefs to put yourself on the gurney? Are you comfortable enough in your faith to put it all on the line?

All in, all the time begins with active goals

Benjamin Franklin made a list of traits he either wanted to lose or wanted to cultivate. Then he graded himself on his progress or regression every day. Not yearly, weekly or monthly, but every day.

His question to himself was, "Did I get closer to accomplishing my goals, or did I lose ground today?"

Franklin chose to focus on accomplishing his goals. He was all in. He was committed enough to keep his goals in view and take a step forward every day.

Writing down and measuring progress toward your goals is not "old school." It's your first step to becoming the person you want to be. Written goals — personally set, continually visualized and important enough to pay the price for success — often mysteriously come true.

Proverbs describes the principle of moving beyond your thoughts and into action: "*Though good advice lies deep within the heart, a person with understanding will draw it out.*"[2]

What are your personal, professional and spiritual goals? If you answer, "I don't know," then you will go somewhere you also don't know. Don't leave the decision to luck. That will not help you become the person you want to be.

Knowing you are not where God wants you feels miserable. The worst thing to do is to stand half in where you are.

Letting go so you can move forward

Sometimes you have to let go of relationships keeping you from being all in. Of course, you want this decision to be your last resort, but it might have to happen.

It is tough to let go of a relationship. They involve your emotions and, often, your family; it is a tough conversation to leave a comfortable place. However, if someone or something is holding you back from becoming who you want to be, you need to move on.

Jesus taught the value of having people around you to encourage you: "*God has combined the members of the body … but that its parts should have equal concern for each other. If one part suffers, every part suffers with it; if one part is honored, every part rejoices with it.*"[3] Spend your energy with encouragers. No substitute exists for being with people who will suffer and rejoice with you. As a friend of mine says, "Even the Lone Ranger could not do it alone."

Let go of the negative, cynical people preventing you from becoming the person you want to be. They will drain you the way one bad battery will drain all the other batteries in a flashlight. Eventually, you cannot tell which battery brought the good batteries down. Encouragers will charge your battery. Negative, cynical people will drain your battery. Love all people, but do not let anyone keep you from becoming the person you want to be.

But, what about your spouse? Is there ever a time to let go? Your marriage is a divine covenant before God. Unless you are in danger, don't let go of your spouse. Go to the ends of the earth to protect and restore the relationship with your spouse. Letting go of a spouse may be an easy short-term solution to a problem, but it is not a viable option most of the time. Work your way diligently through your situation, and let go only if you have used every resource to make your marriage work. Every resource. Your marriage and family are worth the hard work it takes to keep them together.

Serve

All-in, all-the-time Christians serve others. Jesus' blueprint for service included caring for others by addressing individual needs and teaching them in understandable ways. Jesus set the example for servant leadership.

He served others to the extent He gave His life away. Jesus washed His disciples' feet and told them, "*Now that I, your Lord and Teacher, have washed your feet, you also should wash one another's feet. I have set you an example that you should do as I have done for you.*"[4]

The Christian model is to ***serve*** rather than to ***use*** — give rather than take.

Three specific ministries call you to serve: Ministers of encouragement to others; ministers of reconciliation to those with splintered relationships; and ministers of attendance in your local church.

Serving in a local church is a requirement for consistent spiritual growth. It is your soil for growing a healthy spiritual life.

You can listen to some great sermons on television and on the web. You can listen while you cook or get ready for the big game. You may justify that listening to a service online or watching one on television are fulfilling your attendance ministry, but they do not. Solitary time on the lake doesn't either. Although you can have a spiritual experience in all those scenarios, they do not replace attending your local church.

Nothing replaces your involvement, face–to-face with other people. You have to be there. If you want to hear more from God, know more about God or walk closer to God, you have to go where His Word is taught. Regularly. Weekly. All the time.

Several times for me, a sermon or encouraging word positively changed my life. You never know when those special moments will come. I may not have wanted to go to church that particular day, but if I had not been there, I would have missed out on a life-changing moment. I had to be there to receive my gift of encouragement or renewed hope.

The frustrating church

You can't have an "I'm out pass," even when your church life gets frustrating. When my church life becomes frustrating, I know I need to hitch up, not flee. I need to do more, not run away from what needs doing.

You may have had issues with your church in the past. Those issues even may be well founded. We've all had disappointments — maybe in legalism, processes or disagreements with leaders of the church. I understand. I have been there, too.

If you look closely enough, you will find a reason to be unhappy in your church; no church is perfect. Don't allow yourself to rationalize your absence.

The church is God's house, and you are one of God's people; therefore, you need involve yourself in a local church. Find one to go all in, all the time, and serve your local community.

The more you love God, the more you will want to know Him. It seems to me that regardless of the church's imperfections, it's almost impossible to love God but not like church.

What about money?

Wait! I can hear your thoughts, "He just finished writing about church, and now he is writing about money?" You don't need to check my biography; I am not on any church staff.

I simply think both subjects are important to being all in, all the time.

I have seen families destroyed by finances. Some families split because members don't agree on the money's distribution, even though there was more than enough for everyone. Other families struggle and argue about how to make ends meet after each payday.

How you allocate your money is a major decision in every family, during every quarter of your life. The way you spend your money reveals the person you want to be.

Many people believe if they had more money, they would be happier. While that sounds good, more money might actually destroy them. You have heard of numerous lottery winners' lives turned upside down after winning. Winning destroyed their lives.

Don't get me wrong. Money does not destroy people. Many Christians are blessed financially and are living in God's will. In fact the bible clearly expresses the importance of providing for our families: "*If anyone does not provide for his relatives, and especially for his immediate family, he has denied the faith and is worse than an unbeliever.*"[5]

So, money is not the problem; the issue is how you handle your money.

Does a correlation exist between money and happiness? A 2012 Gallup poll revealed that seven of the top 10 countries with the happiest people were in Latin America. The socioeconomic status there is nowhere near the same ballpark as the United States. The U.S. ranked 32.[6]

Decide what you want from that statistic. My point is that measuring a person's success or happiness solely on their financial portfolio is false and temporary. You can go back to the days of Solomon and see the same result: "*Whoever loves money, never has money enough; whoever loves wealth is never satisfied with his income. This too is meaningless.*"[7] If you judge success only by your possessions, you measure against what Solomon called meaninglessness.

Handling money is not a new challenge. Jesus talked about money in His parables more than any other subject. Sixteen of Christ's 38 parables addressed money. He knew the temptations that accompany money.

Everyone has to choose how to handle money; few people have enough to do everything they want. Paul provided instructions to Timothy: "*Teach those who are rich to not be arrogant or put their hope in wealth, which is so uncertain, but put their hope in God, who richly provides us everything for our enjoyment.*"[8] All-in Christians intentionally prioritize how they manage their money.

Many good money management "systems" exist, but I think they all include four simple steps:

1. **Believe that all your finances are from God, and begin with God in your allocation.**
   "*But remember the Lord your God, for it is he who gives you the ability to produce wealth, and so confirms his covenant, which he swore to your ancestors, as it is today.*"[9] And in the New Testament: "*Don't be deceived, my dear brothers. Every good and perfect gift is from above, coming down from the Father of the heavenly lights who does not change like shifting shadows.*"[10]

I believe in tithing. Tithing is taking the first 10 percent of your income and giving it to promoting God's kingdom. It is not a new concept. "*A tithe of everything from the land, whether grain from the soil or fruit from the trees, belongs to the Lord; it is holy to the Lord.*"[11]

Tithing is not an outdated concept, either. Tithing your first fruit reveals your first priority.

If you give because you think your gift will help you gain more financially, you are not really giving. You are trading. The Bible says to give not reluctantly or under compulsion, for God loves a cheerful giver. There is no mention of a cheerful trader. I discovered that the more I gave financially, the more I have to give in other ways. Getting something in return may be a wonderful side benefit but should never be the reason for giving. You give because you choose to give.

To make tithing real in your life, you must make different choices. Giving God 10 percent of what He has given you and spending 90 percent of it is a good choice. If you have trouble tithing, I recommend you tithe the same way you pay taxes — electronically. You never see the money and do not have the option to spend your first 10 percent anywhere else.

2. **Live beneath your means.**

   Most people tend to live at a level that matches their income. Some spend even more than their income. When an unexpected expense comes along, chaos erupts. It is up to you to be content and live beneath your means.

   One of the great temptations today is debt. Credit cards, mortgages and car loans are all easy to get but tough to pay back. How you manage your debt affects your peace. Don't fall into the trap of easy money; there is no such thing.

Chasing what others have and pushing your budget to the max is a never-ending run on a treadmill.

3. **Make saving a portion of your money a priority.**
   You frequently will be blindsided by some unknown, unexpected expense. Don't be surprised; you know it is coming, so plan for it. The unexpected should be budgeted just like your house payment. It may be best to have your savings deducted electronically, too.

   Proverbs teaches: "*Go to the ant, you sluggard; consider its ways and be wise! It has no commander, no overseer or ruler, yet it stores its provisions in summer and gathers its food at harvest.*"[12]

   Expect big events to cost big money: Cars, homes, college education, weddings and retirement. You must plan for those events years in advance. Money to fund them will not be lying around for when you need it. A disciplined plan prepares you for both the expected and unexpected big events.

4. **Create your financial plan together.**
   Your financial plan should be a joint venture with your spouse and completely transparent. The Bible tells us three times that a man and his wife become one.[13] Everything should be together — without separate accounts, hidden assets or a money stash. Financial surprises are one of the greatest disrupters of marital harmony. Keep your financial books open to each other.

It is not easy to save money, especially if you begin with your entire paycheck. If you begin each month with 70 percent of your income, you can have peace with money. Give 10 percent to God, save 10 percent, spend 10 percent any way you want for vacations, etc., and live on the remaining 70 percent. You can do that: 70-10-10-10.

This is not an easy plan for most to implement. You may have to adjust your decisions, but spending your money wisely will help you become the person you want to be and help you achieve financial peace. Even if you can't begin with 70-10-10-10, try 85-5-5-5 and work your way to 70-10-10-10.

If you, along with your family, plan for financial peace you can obtain it. Without a plan, financial peace will probably never happen. Begin with God, live beneath your means, save some money, and create your financial plan together.

Summary

The all-in, all-the-time Christians' role is to obey God and serve others. There is no scarcity of feet to wash. Many times, the stumbling block to other people's commitment is your own unwillingness to do what needs to be done.

The direction we have been provided is clear: "*Love the Lord your God with all your heart and with all your soul and with all your mind and with all your strength; and your neighbor as yourself.*"[14]

That is an all-in — not lukewarm, not part-time, and not halfway — all-the-time commitment to Christ. You can't please God, be happy and do good things without being all in, all the time.

When you are all in, you have done everything you can do. Trust God that everything else will take care of itself.

Questions for Discussion

- ✦ Do you have any relationships preventing you from being all in, all the time?
- ✦ Why is it necessary to be involved in a local church?
- ✦ Do you have any spiritual goals you are working toward?
- ✦ Living on 70 percent. Is that realistic? Could 70-10-10-10 work for you?
- ✦ Why is full disclosure with your spouse important?

PART THREE

Preparing Others for Their Second Quarter

"Teach these things and insist that everyone learn them.
Don't let anyone think less of you because you are young.
Be an example to all believers in what you say,
in the way you live, in your love,
your faith, and your purity."
– 1 TIMOTHY 4: 11-12 (NLT)

chapter 11

Listen for Your Call

"... we constantly pray for you, that our God may count you worthy of his calling, and that by his power he may fulfill every good purpose of yours and every act prompted by your faith."
– 2 THESSALONIANS 1:11

Moses: ***Who am I, that I should go?***	— Exodus 3:11
Isaiah: ***Here am I, Send me!***	— Isaiah 6:8
Paul: ***Who are you, Lord?***	— Acts 9: 5

God's call is different for everyone. "*Each one should use whatever gift he has received to serve others, faithfully administering God's grace in its various forms.*"[1]

Every Christian will be called to do something special. Some, like Moses, might question why. Others, like Isaiah, might have prepared for the moment. And some might be like Paul, who had to be thinking, "Are you kidding me?"

Most of us can relate to all three reactions. God's call is irrevocable.

"*For God's gifts and his call can never be withdrawn.*"[2] That is the good news. It's never too late to follow God's call.

However, if you choose to not accept his gift and his call, He will use someone else. That person will enjoy the blessing for following His call. That blessing should be yours.

The Challenge

The world situation today is strikingly similar to the time when God called Moses to lead the Israelites out of the wilderness.

> "*I have indeed seen the misery of my people in Egypt. I have heard them crying out because of their slave drivers, and I am concerned about their suffering. So now I am sending you to Pharaoh to bring my people the Israelites out of Egypt.*"[3]

Now, as then, many people are miserable; they are crying out, and God is concerned because He loves us. The message is this: We need more God-centered people in every profession.

Pre-qualified

Regardless of the mission for which God calls you, the urgency of His call is the same as it was to Moses more than 3,000 years ago. America needs Christians to make a difference in our businesses, churches, schools and homes.

Many Christians hesitate to share the Good News of Christ. They might not feel qualified or trained, or they might not be willing to accept the risk. They might feel afraid of the extra responsibilities to come their way. Some may feel "in over their head."

That's okay. God uses whomever he chooses. You have been prequalified for your special call. Do you think Mary thought she was qualified to carry the Son of God? How about David — was he in over his head in battling a giant?

What about the apostles? Did any of them fit the job description of spreading the good news to all people? What about Saul? Was he the obvious choice to become a passionate follower of Christ?

The answer to all those questions is no. Every one of them probably thought they were in over their heads — the same way you might feel.

And you might never know what God has in store for you or some of the people you influence.

Unknown influence

You might never have heard of Mordecai Ham; most people haven't. He was a farm boy from the hills of Southern Kentucky who gave his life to Christ at a young age. He became an evangelist and was "on the circuit" for more than 30 years. He delivered one of his messages in Charlotte, North Carolina, in November 1934; a young man, who was one of many in the congregation, gave his life to Christ that night.

That young man was Billy Graham. Dr. Graham arguably has had as much influence on the Christian movement in America as anyone in history. Who knows who God would have used if it were not for Mordecai Ham. But Mordecai Ham was the person God called — a simple person living his calling led one of the greatest Christian leaders of all time to Christ.

If we allow God to work through us, we may never know the impact of our obedience.

A price to pay

As with anything of value, you will pay a price to become the person you want to be. Leaving your comfort zone, accepting additional responsibilities and being held accountable for your actions are part of that price.

Moses knew the price God was asking him to pay. Imagine how Moses felt when God announced he had chosen him to be the leader.

"Me? Lead your people? Ha! I am just a shepherd. I am perfectly content to tend my father-in-law's flock. The sheep don't talk back. I get them where they need to go by using this staff, and they never complain. I enjoy what I do. It doesn't take much effort. I just lead sheep. I don't want to lead the people. Besides, I don't think I would be any good at it, anyway."

He also might have said, "Okay, I need to convince God I'm not the guy for this job. Maybe he'll show some mercy and release me from this leading-his-people concept."

We're no different from Moses; we have our comfort zones. Moses felt so comfortable, he hesitated to take a risk. Leading the Israelites would mean a real and uncomfortable exit. In his efforts to wiggle out of this overwhelming request from God, Moses came up with five pretty good reasons he wasn't the man for the job.[4] Do any of the following excuses sound familiar?

Lord, I Am Not Qualified. "I am just a homeboy shepherd tending sheep for my father-in-law. I've never led people anywhere, and, besides, that's an awesome responsibility."

Few of us accept the responsibility of God's calling without feeling overwhelmed and frightened. We are all "in over our heads" if we try following God's calling alone. God answered Moses' objection with the simple statement: "*I will be with you.*" Then God gave a vision of the result: "*When you have brought the people out of Egypt, you will worship God on this mountain.*"

Moses might have answered, "When I have brought the people out of Egypt? Wait, I am not through with my argument. That was just my first objection." And like you and I would, he readily made another excuse.

But, Lord, I Am Not Trained. Moses felt unprepared for the role God was asking him to accept. He didn't realize God had been preparing him throughout his life. He had been an Egyptian prince; others did everything for him. As a shepherd, no one did anything for him. Now, God was asking him to use all of his experiences and allow God to work through him.

God answered his objection: "*Say I am who I am. I am sent me to you.*" Once again God looked to the future and told Moses what would happen: "*The elders of Israel will listen to you.*"

If your path is God's will, He will provide your needs.

Moses' next strategy was to personalize the risk: **But, Lord, This Is a Risk for You and Me**. By this time, Moses must have had some clue that his excuses weren't working, so he tried to spread the risk to include God. "*What if they do not believe me or listen?*"

God answered with undeniable proof that Moses was the right person for the job, changing Moses' staff to a snake, making Moses' hand leprous, and then restoring both.

All changes in responsibilities and in life itself, involve risks. What are these risks? Looking foolish, making bad decisions, losing pride and being held to a higher standard ... for starters.

Christians have far more exposure to risk than others, but the greater risk is *not* following God's call for you.

God has commanded all Christians to lead, regardless of job titles or responsibilities. Refusing to respond to God's call makes you miserable until you accept the risk and trust God to provide.

Then Moses delivered the mother of all excuses — the excuse he thought he could not overcome: **But, Lord, I Physically Can't Do It.** Moses was feeling the way you might feel about the demands of being called to a new role.

He did not have a natural gift for his call. "*I am slow of speech and tongue.*"

You have to admit that was a good excuse. Moses was not a good communicator. Good verbal communication is basic equipment if you're going to be a strong leader. Imagine his discomfort. He had been alone with a wooden staff leading sheep that never talked back. Now he would be dealing with people — leading his human flock —– who thought on their own and did talk back. He was chosen to lead God's people out of Egypt?

I am not sure anyone would have been completely comfortable with that call. But for someone who could not speak well, that might have been a little too far beyond his ability to comprehend how he could do what needed to be done. Everyone knows the stress of having to speak in front of a group of people. Either you have the talent to speak in public or you don't. Moses didn't.

But once again, God provided the answer. Instead of healing Moses' speech impediment, God sent Aaron to be Moses' spokesman. Isn't it interesting that God chose to change a staff to a snake and make a hand leprous and restore them, yet chose not to heal Moses' speech?

Without a doubt, God could have made Moses an eloquent, strong communicator to lead His people. Instead, God let Moses be like all of us; God used his weaknesses to make him a better person and leader.

But, Lord, Please Send Someone Else. By this time, Moses was desperate. He had used all of his excuses, and God had overcome every obstacle. Moses tried his last appeal to God: "*O Lord, please send someone else to do it.*"

Moses was begging for someone else — anyone else — to be the chosen leader. He did not feel confident he could do the job; he was looking at the challenge from his perspective. God was looking at Moses from *God's* perspective and was totally confident.

"Take your staff and go!" God said. You are the man. You are God's man.

Out of excuses, Moses finally resigned his shepherd job and obeyed the Lord. Then … "*Moses and Aaron brought together all the elders of the Israelites, and Aaron told them everything the Lord said to Moses. He also performed the signs before the people, and they believed. And when they heard that the Lord was concerned about them and had seen their misery, they bowed down and worshipped.*"[5]

Just as with Moses, God has called you to His holiness, and God is going to do all the work through you.

He just wants you to accept His call.

Summary

God uses whomever he chooses. He may not call the most obvious, well-equipped person to do the work, but He has prequalified those he calls; He will provide them the equipment, skills and other resources to do the job.

Most of the people in the Bible whom He chose to do great things did not fit the job description of the roles they were chosen to do. Mary, Moses, David, the Apostles, Saul — they were all in over their heads, but God did the impossible through each of them.

God continues to do the impossible through people like you and me. He calls those who are imperfect, unsure, untrained, afraid of failure and unable to understand why God has called them to lead. God calls CEOs, vice presidents, supervisors, team leaders, individual contributors, schoolteachers, principals, students, husbands, wives, sons and daughters, priests and pastors to be role models for all people.

Whatever he calls you to do, He will empower you to do it well.

When you embark on God's call, you are on a serious journey. Rely heavily on prayer and your trusted advisors to make the best decisions you can to become the person you want to be.

Living your call is required for living life to the fullest; you make that choice. Wherever God calls you, He calls you to be your very best. "*I urge you to live a life worthy of the calling you have received.*"[6] Jesus taught us to "go and do" not to "sit and stay." The next move is yours. If you do not answer God's call, He will call someone else.

The blessing will pass to them.

Waiting for perfect conditions to accept your call? It won't happen. As the Bible says, "*Whoever watches the wind will not plant; whoever looks at the clouds will not reap.*"[7] Don't wait on things to be perfect before trusting God's direction. Accept the challenge, and respond to the call right now — right where you are.

Questions for Discussion

- ✦ How do you know what God is calling you to do? Have you made any excuses not to accept His call?
- ✦ Have you ever been "in over your head," yet experienced God working through all of your inadequacies?
- ✦ Whose response to their calling do you relate to the most: Moses, Isaiah or Paul?
- ✦ What price would you willingly pay if you confidently knew the eternal results of your "yes?"

chapter 12

Lead the Way

"In everything set them an example by doing what is good."
– Titus 2:7

Look around. People all around you right now are struggling through their second quarter. Pain, sorrow, depression, hopelessness, fear and anxiety — you can see it on the faces of those you meet today.

The good news is … you can be their light. You can bring them hope and encouragement. They can see Jesus in you.

You don't even have to say a word. How you live will speak for you. Most of those around you know your story. They know the pain you've suffered. They remember your heartbreak. They've watched your faith in action. You have provided them hope and inspiration.

You probably already are helping them through their second quarter.

King Christian X and Alexander the Great

During the German occupation of his country in World War II, King Christian X of Denmark noticed the Nazi flag flying over a Danish public building. He immediately called the German commandant of the region and demanded he take the flag down at once. The commandant refused.

"Then a soldier will go and take it down," said the king.

"He will be shot," threatened the commandant.

"I think not," replied the king. "For I shall be the soldier."

Within minutes the flag was down.

More than 2000 years ago, Alexander the Great led his troops across a hot and desolate plain. After 11 days of a grueling advance, he and his soldiers faced death from thirst. However, they pressed on.

At midday, two of his scouts brought Alexander what little water they could find. It hardly filled a cup. His troops stood back and watched; they expected him to drink. Instead, he poured the water into the hot sand.

When questioned, he said, "It's of no use for one to drink when many thirst."

Alexander gave his followers all he had to give at that moment: Example and inspiration.

Whoever you are — if you are a king, great or just an average person — whatever you do, you can provide hope, inspiration and encouragement.

One of your most important responsibilities is to model the

behavior you expect from others and the behavior Christ expects from you.

People follow people

Your example of how you live communicates your values far more clearly than any words you speak. People follow people. People do not follow words.

People follow you. You make a difference — positive or not — at all times.

Everyone learns, from childhood and into maturity, by observing other people's behavior. The question is not, "Are people watching?" The question is, "What are people seeing?" Whether you realize it or not, your example has a positive or negative influence, not just on your family and friends, but on all the people they influence, as well.

Leading by example

After Jesus washed the feet of His disciples, He told them they should lead by example, and he shared the results of their obedience to that command. "*I have set you an example that you should do as I have done for you. I tell you the truth, no servant is greater than his master, nor is a messenger greater than the one who sent him. Now that you know these things, you will be blessed if you do them.*"[1]

Jesus promises blessings to you if you follow His example.

One of the first verses you probably memorized from the Bible was "The Golden Rule." We should treat others the way we would want them to treat us: "*So in everything, do to others what you would have them do to you.*"[2] The golden rule should be your rule in every situation.

Jesus spoke to the Pharisees about the negative influence they had on others: "*Woe to you experts in the law, because you have taken away the key to knowledge. You yourselves have not entered, and you have hindered those who were entering.*"[3] Not only did the Pharisees make bad calls of the law, their example also kept others away from the truth.

At a different time, Jesus instructed the disciples to leave the Pharisees alone: "*Leave them; they are blind guides. If a blind man leads a blind man, both will fall in a pit.*"[4] Many people remain blind to the truths of Christ. Your role is to help open their eyes.

James wrote, "*Who is wise and understanding among you? Let him show it by his good life, by deeds done in the humility that comes from wisdom.*"[5]

The example you set for others to follow illustrates your humility and wisdom.

Paul taught the Corinthians the true meaning of setting an example: "*I urge you to imitate me.*"[6] Think about that. How much power and accountability would you have if you told everyone to imitate you?

Titus was advised, "*In everything set an example by doing what is good. In your teaching show integrity, seriousness and soundness of speech that cannot be condemned, so that those who oppose you may be ashamed because they have nothing bad to say about us.*"[7]

The Bible leaves no room for creative interpretations of leading by example. No exceptions exist when you deal with a bad boss, or for times when travel out of town and no one knows you. You have no exceptions when someone hurts you, when you feel angry or during tough times. There are no exceptions, period.

Give no one any reason to say anything bad about you.

Community role models

Recently, members of one church interviewed the administrators of elementary, middle and high schools surrounding the church. They asked each administrator, "How can our church be of service to your school?"

The interviews were independent, and no one knew how anyone else responded. Yet the answer was the same at every school: "Spend time with the kids, and provide them a role model for their future."

Your role as a Christian does not begin and end at work or in the church. Equally important is the influence you have in your neighborhood. You may be the only person to influence someone to search and find out what makes you complete. You may be the only evidence of Jesus someone will see.

Living your witness

Sometimes it's hard to evaluate the right time and place for sharing the good news of Christ. I feel a little uneasy when I see people on a street corner with megaphones proclaiming the gospel. Maybe they are doing what they are called to do, and God bless them. But I think your most effective witness is right where you spend most of your day.

Nonbelievers at work generally are not interested in a prayer group or Bible study. But you have other methods of witnessing for Christ. The Bible directs you to: "*Be careful to live properly among your unbelieving neighbors. Then even if they accuse you of doing wrong, they will see your honorable behavior, and they will give honor to God when he judges the world.*"[8]

Here is what you can do:

1. **Prepare for the right time.**
   Know what you believe. If you feel unsure about your beliefs, you most likely will not communicate a consistent

message when the opportunity comes along. Study your Bible, be involved in your local church, know your beliefs, and prepare for the time when God provides you an opportunity to witness.

The Bible says, "*Always be prepared to give an answer to everyone who asks you to give the reason for the hope that you have. But do this with gentleness and respect, keeping a clear conscience, so that those who speak maliciously against your good behavior in Christ may be ashamed of their slander.*"[9]

2. **Pray the right time will come.**
   Pray consistently and earnestly for the salvation of each person you know. Lift them up to God by name, and pray that you or someone else will get the opportunity to witness. Follow the attitude of Samuel: "*Far be it from me that I should sin against the Lord by failing to pray for you.*"[10]

   If the right time comes along and you don't know what to say, go to them with someone who can provide the answer they seek. Or, take them to your pastor. Who leads them to Christ is not important — their eternal salvation is.

3. **Live what you believe.**
   Your greatest influence is your behavior. Two things you have complete and absolute control over are what you believe and how you behave. If no difference exists between you and a nonbeliever, why would anyone desire Christ?

   Stay in the Word and in prayer, and the difference will become obvious to all. As Saint Francis of Assisi said, "Preach the gospel at all times and, if necessary, use words."

4. **Wait on God's time.**
   The more you try to force your beliefs on someone, the more likely they will resist. You control your preparation, your prayers and your actions. Be consistent and dedicated in those three, and allow God to control the timing for you to share your faith.

Example by Humility

Whatever your position — whether CEO or summer intern — the ability to show sincere humility is one of the most powerful examples you can set. Exhibiting the humility to respect others' opinions, listen with empathy and seek the wisdom of others is a biblically directed example.

The Christian definition of humility is to be God-focused. It is impossible to be arrogant when you keep your focus on God. The Book of Proverbs provides graphic descriptions of the results of pride and humility:

> *"When pride comes, then comes disgrace, but with humility comes wisdom."*[11]
>
> *"Pride only brings quarrels, but wisdom is found in those who take advice."*[12]
>
> *"The fear of the Lord teaches a man wisdom, and humility comes before honor."*[13]
>
> *"An arrogant man stirs up strife, but he who trusts in the Lord will prosper."*[14]
>
> *"Pride goes before destruction, a haughty spirit before a fall."*[15]

The New Testament is just as clear about humility:

> *"For everyone who exalts himself will be humbled, and he who humbles himself will be exalted."*[16]

> *"Do not think of yourself more highly than you ought, but rather think of yourself with sober judgment, in accordance with the measure of faith God has given you."*[17]

> *"Do nothing out of selfish ambition or vain conceit, but in humility consider others better than yourselves. Each of you should look not only to your own interests, but also to the interests of others."*[18]

There is quite a contrast between pride and humility. You choose:

Pride = disgrace, quarrels and destruction.

Humility = wisdom, honor and exaltation.

Jesus provides our ultimate example of humility. *"And being found in appearance as a man, he humbled himself and became obedient to death — even death on a cross."*[19]

Humility is opposed to your nature but is in keeping with Jesus Christ's example.

Summary

You have no choice about influencing others. You already do. Check the fruit you produce. "… *The fruit of the spirit is love, joy, peace, patience, kindness, goodness, faithfulness, gentleness and self-control.*"[20]

Does that reflect you?

Questions for Discussion

- Can you think of someone in your life who took a courageous stance on an issue? What impact did that have on you?
- What molds your children into becoming who they will become?
- Why is humility so important to Christ?
- What does someone who is "complete" act like?
- What does it mean to consider others better than yourself?

PART FOUR

The Final Score

"For we must all appear before the judgment seat of Christ,
so that each of us may receive what is due us
for the things done while in the body, whether good or bad."
– 2 Corinthians 5:10

Your Ultimate Victory

"Leap for joy, because great is your reward in heaven."
– Luke 6:23

The second quarter will come and go in your life. For most, it will be your defining quarter. In reality, you do not even know when you pass the second quarter and move into your halftime. God's halftime is different from the halftime of life expectancy insurance actuaries use.

We all have a different halftime.

Regardless of the time you have on earth, you are to use what you have for the glory of God. "*But seek first his kingdom and his righteousness, and all these things will be given to you as well. Therefore do not worry about tomorrow, for tomorrow will worry about itself. Each day has enough trouble of its own.*"[1]

God has given you everything you need to get the most out of life's toughest quarter. You are not slaves to sin: "*For we know that our old self was crucified with him so that the body ruled by sin might be done away with, that we should no longer be slaves to sin.*"[2]

You are free to live your life to the fullest.

Living your faith and living life to the fullest is not something you can buy, regardless of your resources. You can't inherit it. No one can give it to you as a present. You cannot steal it from anyone else.

Living life to the fullest is available to all of us:

- ✦ By digging your faith well deep
- ✦ By maintaining your integrity, even when it hurts
- ✦ By being all in, all the time with your commitment to God
- ✦ By prioritizing your priorities
- ✦ By connecting frequently with your Heavenly Father
- ✦ By conquering adversity that comes your way
- ✦ By being optimistic and looking for the best in yourself and others
- ✦ By making positive entrances from difficult exits
- ✦ By standing firm and doing what's right, even when it hurts
- ✦ By being a peacemaker
- ✦ By leading with your positive example
- ✦ By preparing yourself to answer God's personal call to you
- ✦ By trusting God's mercy — again and again

Your influence

Whatever you do, wherever you are, and wherever you go, you have far greater influence than you will ever comprehend. You will come into contact with thousands of people in your lifetime. You influence some of those people, even when you are not aware anyone is watching. You affect everyone you touch.

Think of the people who have made a difference in your life:

Remember that Bible study teacher who influenced you? She sacrificed her time and talent to teach you. She may not remember you, but you remember an encouraging word she gave you at the right moment. That teacher probably never knew the positive impression she made on you. Plaques and awards did not measure her impact.

Remember the schoolteacher you wanted to imitate — the person who helped you by investing extra time with you? That teacher probably never heard about the positive difference he made on you and the way he helped change your life. No test report measured those changes.

Remember the pastor who so eloquently spoke in the pulpit, yet also took the time to get to know you personally? His words and his actions shaped your life; yet, no report at the church measured his impact.

Remember the secretary at work who consistently prayed for the business and the people in the company? Remember how she ministered and soothed the pain when fellow employees went through unexplained problems? There is no annual recognition banquet for her. No one knows the influence she had on you and others.

The traditional ways to measure success and effectiveness do not measure long-term impact. Traditionally, attendance each week might have measured the Bible study teacher's effectiveness. Achievement test scores might have measured the schoolteacher's effectiveness. The distribution of quick and accurate reports might have measured the secretary's performance. Church growth might have measured the pastor's effectiveness.

None of those important people were measured by the impact they had on *your* life.

If they had been concerned only with attendance, grades, reports and church growth, they would not have cared about the difference they had made in others' lives. Fortunately, they did care. They looked beyond the normal measurements and rewards and went out of their way to positively impact your life.

Similarly, traditional "success factors" cannot measure living life to the fullest. The size of your bank account, house and car, your job description, the number of employees you manage, and your income statement cannot measure your life; neither are these things your reward.

Your ultimate victory will come in rewards far beyond what you can imagine.

Set your personal goals, and work to accomplish them. But remember: Regardless of the world's view, no success exists if you lose your family. And you can't have success without a personal relationship with Christ.

"For no one can lay any foundation other than the one already laid, which is Jesus Christ. If any man builds on this foundation using gold, silver, costly stones, wood, hay or straw, his work will be shown for what it is."[3]

There is no success without Christ!

Living life to the fullest requires Christ in the center. *"It is required that those who have been given a trust must prove faithful … it is the Lord who judges me … He will bring to light what is hidden in darkness and will expose the motives of men's hearts. At that time each will receive his praise from God."*[4]

Solomon wrote about enjoying life while understanding our purpose in life. His conclusion was, "*Fear God and keep his commandments, for this is the whole duty of man. For God will bring every deed into judgment, including every hidden thing, whether it is good or evil.*"[5]

Our success comes when we bring glory to God.

Mother Teresa of Calcutta once said, "When it is hard, remember we are not called to be successful but to be faithful. Let no one ever come to you without leaving better and happier. Be the living expression of God's kindness: kindness in your face, kindness in your eyes, kindness in your smile." We need to express God's goodness in everything we do. There is no time to give up.

My final note is to remind you of the ultimate non-negotiable of life.

Your decision to follow Jesus Christ and to lead others to Him is the most important decision you will ever make. As Jesus said, "*What good is it for someone to gain the whole world, yet forfeit their soul?*"[6] Nothing on earth is more valuable than your soul. Following Jesus all in, all the time is living life to the fullest.

No one knows when he is in the fourth quarter of life. David spoke of the shortness of our lives in Psalms: "*As for man, his days are like grass, he flourishes like a flower of the field; and the wind blows over it and it is gone, and its place remembers it no more.*"[7]

Whichever quarter you're in now, your ultimate goal should be as Paul wrote at the end of his productive and fulfilled life: "*I have fought the good fight, I have finished the course, I have kept the faith.*"[8]

What a fabulous epitaph! He seized every moment and passionately pursued God's will for his life.

No remorse. No regrets. All in. All the time.

Thomas Chisholm (1866-1960) lived a relatively obscure life, but he authored a poem based on Lamentations 3:22-23 that is one of my favorite hymns and has been an inspiration to millions:[9]

> Great is thy faithfulness!
> Great is thy faithfulness!
> Morning by morning new mercies I see.
> All I have needed Thy hand hath provided;
> Great is Thy faithfulness, Lord, unto me!
>
> Great is Thy faithfulness, O God my Father;
> There is no shadow of turning with Thee;
> Thou changest not, Thy compassions, they fail not;
> As Thou hast been, Thou forever will be.

He is faithful to you; live faithfully for Him. If you live life to the fullest as an obedient, loving Christian, everyone will see Jesus in you.

Your ultimate victory eventually will arrive when you come face-to-face with the Father who created you, and He holds your hand and says to you, "***Well done, thy good and faithful servant.***"[10]

"May the God of Peace, who through the blood of the eternal covenant brought back from the dead our Lord Jesus, that great shepherd of the sheep, equip you with everything good for doing his will, and may he work in us what is pleasing to him through Jesus Christ, to whom be glory for ever and ever. Amen."[11]

A MESSAGE FROM THE AUTHOR

Thank you for reading this book. The purpose of the book is to provide you a guide as you search through Scriptures for answers to today's issues. I hope it accomplished this for you.

I have found that the answers to all our questions are in the Bible, and it does not take a biblical scholar to understand God's word. It only takes wanting to know and hear. My sincere desire is that the principles expressed in this book will help you become a more effective spouse, friend, worker and believer.

I want to thank my family. This book exposes some of my family's greatest challenges. Through it all, not one person lost his or her faith. That was due in a large part to my late wife, Karen, who lived an incredibly inspiring life for others to see Jesus in her.

I also want to thank my wife Madeline's family. Her late husband, John LeBlanc, served as a wonderful role model for all to see. His positive influence continues to be reflected through Madeline and their children.

Madeline helped me write many sections of this book. Her knowledge of the Bible and her wisdom provided valuable seasoning to the book. Thank you.

My desire is for this book to be the vehicle to expose as many people to Jesus Christ as possible. During the next two weeks, you will have the opportunity to recommend this book to at least 10 friends and associates. I hope you will. Your recommendation could make a life-changing difference.

May God bless you,

ABOUT THE AUTHOR

David and his miracle granddaughter, Elle

David Cottrell is president and CEO of CornerStone Leadership. He is a premier authority on leadership and has worked with many of today's most successful organizations, mentoring leaders to peak performance.

Before founding CornerStone, David held leadership positions with Xerox and FedEx and led the successful turnaround of a Chapter 11 company. An internationally known author, educator and speaker, he has been a featured expert on public television and has shared his leadership philosophy and lessons with more than 400,000 leaders worldwide.

David has authored more than 25 books, selling over 2 million copies. His books are currently translated into 10 languages. He and his wife, Madeline, split their time between Covington, Louisiana, and Boerne, Texas.

He can be reached at info@CornerStoneLeadership.com.

Other Books by David Cottrell

Monday Morning Choices

Monday Morning Mentoring

Monday Morning Motivation

Monday Morning Leadership

Monday Morning Customer Service

Monday Morning Communications

Monday Morning Leadership for Kids

136 Effective Presentation Tips

175 Ways to Get More Done in Less Time

Birdies, Pars, and Bogeys: Leadership Lessons from the Links

Becoming the Obvious Choice

David Cottrell's Collection of Favorite Quotations

Escape from Management Land: A Journey Every Team Wants Their Leader to Take

Listen Up, Customer Service

Listen Up, Leader

Listen Up, Teacher

Leadership . . . Biblically Speaking

Leadership Courage

Management Insights

The Leadership Secrets of Santa Claus

The Manager's Coaching Handbook

The Manager's Communication Handbook

The Manager's Conflict Resolution Handbook

The Nature of Excellence

The Next Level: Leading Beyond the Status Quo

Time!

Tuesday Morning Coaching … Eight Simple Truths to Boost Your Career and Your Life

Winners Always Quit! Seven Pretty Good Habits You Can Swap for Really Great Results

Available at www.**CornerStoneLeadership**.com

NOTES

Introduction

1. Ecclesiastes 1:9-10
2. 1 Corinthians 10:13
3. John 8:32
4. Romans 15:4

Chapter One–
Dig Your Faith Well Deep

1. Hebrews 11:1
2. Hebrews 11:6
3. 2 Timothy 4:7 (emphasis mine)
4. 2 Corinthians 5:7
5. Luke 9:12-17
6. Luke 8:22-25
7. Luke 8:26-39
8. Luke 8:43-48
9. Luke 5:17-26
10. Luke 5:12-15
11. Mark 6:45-52
12. Matthew 9:27-31
13. Matthew 9:33
14. John 11:1-45
15. John 2:1-11
16. Luke 22:49-51
17. John 5:1-6
18. Mark 4:40
19. Hebrews 11:6
20. James 1:2-3
21. Romans 7:15
22. 2 Corinthians 4:8
23. Hebrews 4:13
24. Matthew 25:14-30
25. Romans 8:28
26. Jeremiah 29:11
27. Hebrews 10:24-25
28. 1 Thessalonians 5:11-23 (emphasis mine)
29. Hebrews 11:6
30. Hebrews 11:13

Chapter Two–
Guard Your Integrity

1. New York Times, November 9, 2012
2. James 1:12
3. Proverbs 10:9
4. Romans 12:21
5. Psalm 25:21
6. Ecclesiastes 5:5-6 (NLT)
7. Matthew 5:37
8. Mark 6:21-29
9. 1 Peter 3:15
10. 1 Corinthians 6:19-20
11. Proverbs 13:3 (NLT)
12. James 3:3-11
13. Ephesians 4:29
14. Proverbs 12:19
15. Proverbs 12:22
16. Titus 2:7-8
17. John C. Maxwell, *Developing the Leader Within You* (Nelson, 1993)
18. 1 Peter 3:14
19. 2 Samuel 11:1-25
20. Psalm 51:1-2

Chapter Three –
Prioritize Your Priorities

1. Ephesians 5:15-16
2. 1 Corinthians 14:40
3. David Cottrell, *175 Ways to Get More Done in Less Time* (CornerStone, 2014)
4. Mark 4:38
5. Luke 10:40
6. Ecclesiastes 5:18-20
7. Frederick Reichheld, *The Loyalty Effect* (Harvard Business Press, 1996)
8. Luke 18:1
9. Matthew 6:33 (emphasis mine)

Chapter Four
Take Optimism With You

1. 2 Corinthians 7:4
2. 1 Thessalonians 5:18
3. Titus 2:7-8
4. Matthew 6:27
5. Matthew 6: 34
6. Wells and Matthews, University of Cincinnati, 1990

7. Proverbs 12:25
8. Philippians 4:6
9. Luke 8:9-15
10. Matthew 11:28-30
11. Barna Group Research, 2008
12. Deuteronomy 31:8
13. Ecclesiastes 3:1-12
14. Psalm 139:14 (emphasis mine)
15. Philippians 3:13-14
16. Philippians 4:13
17. 2 Timothy 1:7
18. Philippians 3:10

Chapter Five –
Pray Like There is No Tomorrow

1. Luke 11:1
2. Luke 11:2-4
3. Matthew 6:9-13
4. Romans 12:12
5. Luke 23:42
6. Luke 23:43
7. Ecclesiastes 5:1-2
8. Psalm 46:10
9. Isaiah 30:15
10. Romans 10:17
11. James 1:22-24
12. 2 Timothy 3:16-17
13. 1 Thessalonians 5:19
14. 1 Thessalonians 5:17
15. Luke 18:41
16. 1 Thessalonians 5:18
17. Luke 17:11-18
18. Psalm 37:7
19. Psalm 25:4-5
20. Proverbs 3:13
21. Isaiah 6:8
22. Hebrews 13:8
23. Matthew 26:39
24. 2 Chronicles 7:14
25. Romans 8:26
26. Ephesians 6:18

Chapter Six –
Conquer Adversity When It Strikes

1. Proverbs 24:10
2. Romans 8:28
3. Matthew 11:28-30
4. 1 Corinthians 2:9
5. Matthew 5:4
6. Galatians 6:9
7. Romans 8:38
8. Psalm 34:18
9. Isaiah 55:8-9
10. Proverbs 3:5-6

Chapter Seven –
Move Through Exits, Make Grand Entrances

1. Genesis 37
2. Genesis 37:5-8
3. Genesis 37: 9-11
4. Genesis 50:19-21
5. Genesis 12:1-8
6. Acts 9:1-17
7. Philippians 3:14
8. Galatians 6:9

Chapter Eight –
Stand Firm

1. Judges 7
2. 1 Samuel 17:37
3. Acts 9:23-30
4. Acts 4:1-4
5. Luke 4
6. John 5:1-9
7. 2 Chronicles 20:17
8. Charles Swindoll, *Hope Again*, (Word, 1996)
9. Isaiah 40:31
10. Hebrews 10: 35-36
11. Ephesians 6:13-17

Chapter Nine –
Give Peace a Chance

1. Philippians 4:8
2. 1 Peter 5:7
3. Proverbs 23:23 (LB)
4. Proverbs 18:13
5. Proverbs 18:17
6. 1 Samuel 30:4
7. 1 Samuel 30:6

8. James 1:19-20
9. Matthew 5:9
10. James 3:18
11. Matthew 18:21-22
12. Luke 23:34
13. Ephesians 4:31-32
14. 1 Peter 3:9
15. Romans 3:23
16. Philippians 4:7 (emphasis mine)

Chapter Ten –
Be All In, All the Time

1. Revelations 3:15
2. Proverbs 20:5 (NLT)
3. 1 Corinthians 12:24-26
4. John 13: 14-15
5. 1 Timothy 5:8
6. Michael Weissenstein, "Happiest People on Planet Live in Latin America, Gallup Poll Suggests," Huffington Post, December 19, 2012
7. Ecclesiastes 5:10
8. 1 Timothy 6:17
9. Deuteronomy 8:18
10. James 1:16-17
11. Leviticus 27:30
12. Proverbs 6:6-8
13. Genesis 2:24, Matthew 19:5, Ephesians 5:31
14. Mark 12:30

Chapter Eleven –
Listen For Your Call

1. 1 Peter 4:10
2. Romans 11:29
3. Exodus 3:7, 10
4. Exodus 3:11-4:17
5. Exodus 4:29-30
6. Ephesians 4:1
7. Ecclesiastes 11:4

Chapter Twelve –
Lead the Way

1. John 13:14-15
2. Matthew 7:12
3. Luke 11:52
4. Matthew 15:14
5. James 3:13
6. 1 Corinthians 4:16
7. Titus 2: 6-8
8. 1 Peter 2:12-13 (NLT)
9. 1 Peter 3: 15-16
10. 1 Samuel 12:23
11. Proverbs 11:2
12. Proverbs 13:10
13. Proverbs 15:33
14. Proverbs 18:6
15. Proverbs 16:18
16. Luke 14:11
17. Romans 12:3
18. Philippians 2:3-4
19. Philippians 2:8
20. Galatians 5:22-23

Your Ultimate Victory

1. Matthew 6:33-34
2. Romans 6:6
3. 1 Corinthians 3:11-12
4. 1 Corinthians 4:2-5
5. Ecclesiastes 12:13-14
6. Mark 8:36
7. Psalm 103:15-16
8. 2 Timothy 4:7
9. Thomas Chisholm, *Great is Thy Faithfulness*, (Carol Stream, Illinois, Hope Publishing)
10. Matthew 25:21
11. Hebrews 13:20

Second Quarter Special

$70.00

($145 value!)

All seven hardcover books for one great price!

Package includes:

- *Monday Morning Mentoring*
- *Monday Morning Choices*
- *Tuesday Morning Coaching*
- *The Magic Question*
- *Indispensable!*
- *Monday Morning Leadership for Kids*
- *The Nature of Excellence* Classic Edition (6" x 6")

www.**CornerStoneLeadership**.com

Order additional copies for your Bible study teams

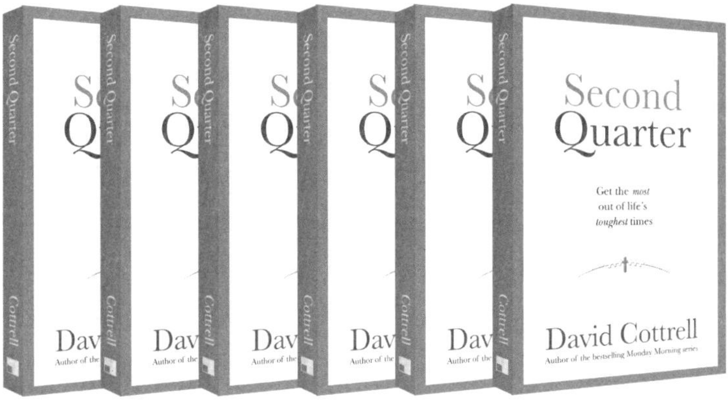

Second Quarter Quantity Discounts	
1-4 copies $19.95	5-9 copies $18.95
10-19 copies $17.95	20 - 99 copies $16.95
100+ copies $14.95	

972.298.8377 www.CornerStoneLeadership.com
P.O. Box 764087, Dallas, TX 75376

We want to hear from you!

Your comments and suggestions are welcomed! Please let us know how your church or organization is using *Second Quarter* and the impact it is making in lives in your community.

Please write to us at info@CornerStoneLeadership.com.

Thank you for reading *Second Quarter!*

We hope it has assisted you in your quest for personal and spiritual growth. CornerStone Leadership's mission is to fuel knowledge with practical resources that will accelerate your success and life satisfaction!

Start a crusade –
have the courage to learn, the vision to lead,
and the passion to share.